THE FAMILY
AT CHURCH

How Parents Are Tour Guides for Joy

20 DAYS TO TRANSFORM
Your Local Church Experience

SCOTT T. BROWN

The Family at Church
20 Days to Transform Your Local Church Experience

First Printing: November 2020

Church & Family Life
220 South White St., Wake Forest, NC 27587
www.churchandfamilylife.com

ISBN: 978-1-62418-062-0

Cover Design by Steadfast Design Firm
Typography by Justin Turley

Printed in the United States of America

ENDORSEMENTS

"One of the most important things every Christian parent must do is inculcate in our children a deep and lasting love for the church. Scott Brown's latest book, *The Family at Church*, shows how to do this—and why it's a delightful task, not a drudgery. This is one of the best manuals on Christian parenting I have ever studied."

—*Phil Johnson is Executive Director of* Grace to You *and elder at Grace Community Church, Sun Valley, California.*

"We are so grateful that during our growing up years our father helped to foster a love for the local church. He helped us to love the saints, the Word of God, worshiping together and recognizing the value of being intimately involved in each other's lives. We believe this book will be a helpful tool to give you fresh eyes to see the benefits of the church. It will impress on your hearts her sacred importance. If there was ever a time for instilling in our children a love and appreciation for the local church, it is now. With our culture questioning the importance of many church fundamentals, it is up to us to inspire our children to see its value, beauty and holiness in the eyes of God."

—*Kelly, Blair, David and Claudia, children of Scott and Deborah Brown*

"Scott Brown loves the church and the family. It is no surprise, then, that he has written these devotions designed to help parents train their children to treasure the local church. These twenty short chapters cultivate sweet anticipation that in the church we find God's richest blessing: fellowship with Him through Jesus Christ by the Holy Spirit."

—*Dr. Joel R. Beeke is President of Puritan Reformed Theological Seminary, and pastor at the Heritage Reformed Congregation, Grand Rapids, Michigan.*

"Every home is to be the frontline for Christian discipleship with a strong involvement in the ministry of the local church. How that mutual participation is worked out requires much insight and wisdom. Scott Brown supplies the help we need. Writing as a devoted father and seasoned pastor, Scott provides well-measured counsel in these pages. If your family wants to maximize a most positive experience in the body of Christ, I am sure you will be helped by this book."

—Dr. Steven Lawson is President of One Passion Ministries, Teaching Fellow with Ligonier Ministries, Professor of Preaching and Dean of the Doctor of Ministry program at The Masters Seminary.

"When I read this book, I feel as if I am eavesdropping on a conversation with a man who has thought and labored much as both a father and a pastor. In these pages we are reminded of the significant opportunities God has given us as families and churches. Here the author shows us how the local church, God's 'divinely designed ecosystem,' is the most important entity for the family's growth in a gospel-oriented joy."

—John Snyder is a pastor at Christ Church New Albany in New Albany, Mississippi. He is author of the "Behold Your God" series.

"I'm glad well-known people are recommending this book. I'm grateful they would lend their names to it. But I am the perfect person to commend it to you. Why? Because Scott and Deborah started teaching Janet and me these things before we even married, and it pointed us in a direction which has been invaluable in bringing up our children in the training and admonition of the Lord. The Brown family practiced what Scott is preaching in this book. This is what he has been preaching as long as I've known him (we met in 1990), and I have several decades of reaping the benefits. You can too."

—Jason Dohm is a pastor at Sovereign Redeemer Community Church, Youngsville, North Carolina.

"In *The Family at Church: How Parents are Tour Guides for Joy*, Scott Brown provides a profoundly biblical roadmap of encouragement for parents. Not only is it biblical, but it is also wonderfully practical. The family and the church are both institutions that were established by God, and Scott Brown highlights their interconnectedness in this valuable resource for parents and families."

> —*Anthony R. Mathenia is a pastor at Christ Church Radford and member of the Board of Directors of HeartCry Missionary Society.*

"Oh, that parents would capture the heart of this book, and demonstrate a true passionate love for God and His worship in the assembly of the saints! What a critical word for such a time as this! If there is anything needed in a day of spiritual dearth, that would be a love for the Lord and His body. This will be the basis for family and church reformation in our day."

> —*Kevin Swanson is President of Generations and a pastor at Reformation Church, Elizabeth, Colorado.*

"Raising children in the nurture and admonition of the Lord is not only the duty of parents, but their joy. You simply cannot fulfill the delightful responsibility without the church of Jesus Christ. May the truth with this compact book equip you as you labor to see the coming generation following the Lord Jesus Christ."

> —*Jared Longshore is a pastor at Grace Baptist Church, Cape Coral, Florida and board member and Vice President of Founders Ministries.*

"Reading this book felt like cool water in the dessert, shade on a hot summer's day, or a comfortable pillow at night. I finished the book refreshed, revived, grateful to serve a Great King, and challenged to be a better husband and father! I believe 'The Family at Church' is one of the most important books of this generation. Every church leader and every Christian family needs to read this book!"

—*Carlton C. McLeod is Senior Pastor at Calvary Reformation Church, Chesapeake, Virginia.*

"In his extremely practical book entitled *The Family at Church: How Parents are Tour Guides for Joy,* author Scott Brown gives us valuable pastoral advice for helping families with children of all ages to love, enjoy, and benefit from the local church. Having read it, I am compelled to get this excellent new work into the hands of all of my people. I am delighted that this volume is available and believe that if its lessons are implemented, it will do much good for generations to come. May God grant it to be so!"

—*Pastor Rob Ventura is a pastor at Grace Community Baptist Church, North Providence, Rhode Island.*

"Scott Brown believes that God designed the family as the place where children are best led to Christ and nurtured as his disciples, but God never meant for parents to do this alone—families need the local church. I am so thankful for this useful resource, and I hope every Christian parent will read this book and commit to making the local church the center of their lives."

—*Scott Aniol is Associate Professor of Worship at Southwestern Baptist Theological Seminary and founder of Religious Affections Ministries.*

"Scott Brown has written a very practical guide for turning a mundane day at church into a day of joyful transformation for the whole family. I highly recommend this book. May God use this book to bring God's people to long for the courts of God and to find great joy in God's presence."

—*Phillip Kayser is a pastor at Dominion Covenant Church, Omaha, Nebraska.*

"Scott Brown loves the church. He loves the family. In *The Family at Church*, both of these loves shine brightly. He tells how the church can and should strengthen the family, and how the family can and should strengthen the church. He explains their interdependence. Read it. Practice it. Pass its lessons on to your children and your children's children. You, and they, will be blessed."

—*E. Calvin Beisner is founder and national spokesman for The Cornwall Alliance for the Stewardship of Creation.*

"This book could not have come at a better time. The glorious church of Jesus Christ has been labeled as 'non-essential' by a world that has become preoccupied with a declared pandemic. This book is a helpful resource for parents to better understand the importance of the local church and helpfully points to concrete ways that parents can teach the rising generation the beauty, the glory, and the value of the Bride of Jesus Christ. "

—*Mike Davenport is a pastor at Hope Baptist Church, Wake Forest, North Carolina.*

"Scott Brown has done the church of Christ an enormous service in writing *The Family at Church*. Using both a theology of the church and the family, Scott has shown how Scripture requires and equips all parents to the work of raising their children in a godly fashion. *The Family at Church* is a refreshing call to Christians to love those very institutions which are so threatened by modern culture."

—*Matt Holst is a pastor at Shiloh Presbyterian Church, Raleigh, North Carolina.*

"In recent years there has been an encouraging recovery of the biblical doctrine of the Christian family, but without a proper understanding of the church of Christ, true family integration into the church will not be attained. We should love the church and teach our children to love her, which is what this book is designed to do. Its short chapters are founded on biblical principles and full of practical instruction. It is a wonderfully helpful tool for families and congregations."

—*Gavin Beers is a pastor at Cornerstone Presbyterian Church, Mebane, North Carolina.*

"This family field guide not only builds a foundation for the local church as being a priority in the hearts and schedules of Christians, but gives practical counsel as to how parents can better prepare, disciple and manage their children for local church worship."

—*Bernie Diaz is a pastor at Christ Community Church, Pembroke Pines, Florida.*

"Any tour guide worth his salt has been equipped to know the best places to take his customers that will fill them with joy and wonder. This type of tour guide is exactly what Scott Brown is preparing his readers to be. Parents, if you are looking for both a biblical and practical guide to help you joyfully train your children in righteousness, I would encourage you to open the pages of this book."

—*Adam Burrell is an Associate Pastor at Pray's Mill Baptist Church, Douglasville, Georgia.*

"In this book, Scott Brown does what is largely missing in many books on the subject of the local church. He does an excellent job of helping God's people see the beauty and the glorious nature of the local church. If we are serious about retaining the next generation in our churches, we need to inspire them to love the church. This book will help you, your family, and your church recover and return to the right view of the household of God."

—*Malamulo Chindongo is a pastor at Antioch Baptist Church, Blantyre, Malawi.*

"What a wonderful treasury of practical counsel for the practice of keeping our children with us in church Scott Brown has given us here! I could not agree more that children from a very young age should be with their parents in church and trained not only to be un-distracting to others but to worship God themselves. I am also very enthusiastic about Scott's vision for keeping and overseeing children in church. I hope this becomes a great tool for parents who have the biblical vision for having their children in church with them."

—*Dr. Sam Waldron, Dean and Professor of Systematic Theology at Covenant Baptist Theological Seminary.*

"In this helpful book by Scott Brown you will see why it is important that you treat the gathering of the church for what it is, the most spectacular gathering the family will participate in all week. Read this with your spouse and be encouraged. Read this with others and be strengthened. Pastor, get a copy of this book into the hands of every family you know."

—*Paul Thompson is a pastor at Eastside Baptist Church, Twin Falls, Idaho.*

"As a pastor, husband and father, I am indebted to Scott Brown for providing parents who wish to cultivate joy in their home toward the local church with a practical, biblically-based devotional that is sympatric to the business of real family life. Start the twenty-day tour today! Moms and Dads, don't pass this up."

—*Doug Barger is a pastor at Christ Reformed Baptist Church, New Castle, Indiana.*

"The Scriptures teach us that the church of Jesus is central to the Christian life. We cannot devote ourselves to any group of greater importance in this life than the local church. Scott Brown does an excellent job of pointing out the need for the family to attend church together with a desire to invest in the lives of children—training them in the gospel of Jesus for the glory of God and their ultimate joy in the faith."

—Josh Buice is a pastor at Pray's Mill Baptist Church, Douglasville, Georgia and Founder and President of G3 Ministries and the G3 Conference.

"In over 25 years of ministering to families, one of the most common struggles I hear is related to navigating church involvement. Because of problems plaguing churches in the West, many are adopting a low view of church. Scott Brown takes a pastoral and biblical look at how families can engage the church with reverence, joy and humility. It is my hope that many parents will find direction and guidance through this important work."

—Israel Wayne is an author, speaker and President of Family Renewal.

"How your children turn out in their adult years depends largely on the interplay they experience between the family and the church in their formative years. That is a loaded statement! What Scott Brown does in this 20-day family field guide is to mine the depths of that statement. I commend this book to you. In reading it you will see how you can maximize the gospel-centered and joy-filled benefits for both the family and the church."

—Conrad Mbewe is a pastor at Kabwata Baptist Church, Lusaka, Zambia.

"What a relevant and necessary resource! There are books on churches and there are books on families, but this is the best resource I've seen bringing God's two most important institutions together within the same pages. You'll see the intersection and overlap between the church and family like you never have before. With helpful discussion questions at the end of each chapter, you can immediately begin applying the wonderful information."

—*Scott LaPierre, is a pastor at Woodland Christian Church, in Woodland Washington.*

"This book is a biblically faithful initiative to facilitate the flourishing of the synergy between the two indispensable institutions that Almighty God has ordained for the growth and sustainability of humanity: the family and the church. In a generation in which there is widespread apostasy as well as the official promotion of perversion by entrenched establishment voices, this bold clarion call for the edification, efficacy and the essential collaboration of these two institutions is timely and welcomed."

—*Hensworth W C Jonas*
Presiding Elder, Central Baptist Church and Executive Director, East Caribbean Baptist Mission (St. John's, Antigua & Barbuda)

TABLE OF CONTENTS

THE ONRAMP TO THIS BOOK

CHAPTERS

FOREWORD

Many pastors boast of their love for the church, but their words are often betrayed by their actions. In fact, many appear to love their ministries in the church rather than the church herself. Others seem to love the church as a doctrine or as an invisible and universal ideal. In contrast, Scott Brown is a pastor with a true pastor's heart. He loves the local church and cherishes the most immature and difficult of her members as he does Christ Himself. In fact, I believe that he would be content to see his name and ministry perish and be forgotten if only the church would remain and prosper. Like the Apostle Paul, Scott is jealous for the church with a godly jealousy and his high desire is to present her to Christ as a pure virgin (II Corinthians 11:2). Also, like Paul, Scott is weak when the church is weak and intensely concerned when she is led to sin (II Corinthians 11:29). Thus, the reader may rest assured that this brief work is written by a man who loves Christ and loves His church. Even Scott's devotion to the doctrine and praxis of the biblical family has always had a higher purpose—to strengthen and beautify Christ's bride.

Having recommended the author, I may now recommend the book. Although the work is replete with doctrine, it is primarily a plea for us who believe to hold the local church, her ministers, her gathering, and the Lord's Day in the highest esteem and to delight in them as a grace or gift from God. In this book you will not find a hint of pragmatism. There are no marketing methods borrowed from the worldly. There are no innovative church-growth strategies created by those who do not understand the Scriptures or the power of God. There is only the call for the individual believer to see the church as Christ sees her and to delight in her as He does. There is a plea to turn from the near infinite distractions that surround us and focus upon the beauty of Christ's bride and to hear the trumpet blast announcing a weekly jubilee or sabbath rest for the people of God. Especially noteworthy is Scott's graceful encouragement to teach our children to delight in the Lord's Day and to set it apart as a day of rest, reflection, and re-creation (i.e. restoration).

It is for all these reasons and more that I recommend this concise, yet thoughtful and profound work. If your private devotions, spiritual growth, and familiar relationships are on mark, and yet, you find yourself with a sense of being incomplete or wanting, you just may find your answer in giving greater attention to the fellowship of the saints and to the Lord's Day on which they gather.

—Paul Washer

A FAMILY FIELD GUIDE <u>TO THE</u> LOCAL CHURCH

I believe that the most important place you ever take your family is a local church. That is why I am casting a vision for how the ministry of a local church is poised to saturate your family with the gospel, expose them to the "whole counsel of God," save their souls, and grow their love for our Lord Jesus Christ. I am writing to parents who are in the midst of raising their children.

You are at a pivotal time in your lives and I'd like to have a conversation with you about your family and your relationship with your local church. I am concerned about the ways Christian people are treating their local churches. Internet-based church life is not helping. I wish I was sitting in your living room so you could see and hear me. I love families and I desire to see them prosper in all the happiness-es of the kingdom of heaven. I believe that local churches are designed by God to assist in this kind of prosperity and happiness.

This book is a *family field guide* to making the most out of local church life. I want you to recognize the treasure of a biblically ordered local church. The experiences God has supplied through local churches provide a family the means for soaking in the whole counsel of God and the treasures of everlasting joy.

Local churches offer dozens of opportunities to orient your family around the knowledge of the graces of the Lord Jesus Christ.

The earlier you get going on this, the sweeter life will be. Now is the time to strengthen your family and your church.

Give your children 10,000 reasons to believe that Jesus Christ is the only Savior and His Word is the only authority. Do it now. Do it through full engagement in local church life.

THE POWER ᴼᶠ CHURCH ᴬᴺᴰ FAMILY LIFE

T he church and the family are the most influential institutions that exist in the world. God created these two institutions for His glory. They are the chief gospel-preaching, life-equipping institutions.

You probably can't do much about the massive movements that are tearing apart the moral and social structure of the world, but you can do something about your family and your local church.

The assumption that runs throughout this book is that the local church is designed by God. I am arguing that there are particular things the church does. True Christians do them week in and week out.

Because of this divine design, families need to make local churches the center of their priorities. I realize that most people who call themselves Christians do not treat local churches like Christians.

HOW ᵀᴼ USE THIS BOOK

TWENTY DAYS TO TRANSFORM YOUR LOCAL CHURCH EXPERIENCE

I encourage you to read this book on a twenty-day schedule to get maximum value. My mission is to give you thinking processes and practices that could improve the impact of the gospel in your family. I am recommending these things to increase joy and strengthen every member of your family.

I wrote this book with short chapters so that you could read a chapter in about 15 minutes. There are discussion questions at the end of each chapter.

There are twenty chapters in this book. There are twenty workdays per month, assuming a five-day work week. If you read one chapter each day during the week, you will finish this book in a month. I believe that if you did that, it could dramatically increase your delight in the Lord and in your local church. The biblical knowledge base and the approach that I am suggesting will make your local church much more invigorating and valuable.

A VISION OF HOPE

In the pages ahead, I am exalting some of the most beautiful gifts that God has given through His church. I am testifying that the gospel is the most powerful force in the world and God has given it to churches and families.

I am writing to cast a vision of hope.

I do not provide every possible solution to every problem you or your children might face in your journey to be faithful church members. This book is not primarily about navigating all the particular problems you are facing in your church. Rather, it is an identification of opportunities. I want to show you how to do your part. I want to help you maximize every ounce of good in your situation.

I want you to see the fields ripe for harvest and to find every possible way to praise God before the rising generation through your local church life.

This is where hope is found. With all the upheaval in the world today, I rest my hope in the power of the gospel working through God's holy institutions. This is an unshakeable vision of hope.

TOUR GUIDES FOR EVERLASTING JOY

The places you take your children will influence them for the rest of their lives. You parents are their tour guides. You should take them places. You *will* take them places. I believe that the most important place you will ever take your children, outside your home, is a local church. I want to help you maximize the sweetness and power of that experience. I want to equip you to be a great tour guide.

God has appointed you as teachers who guide your children through the experiences of this life, "when you sit in your house, when you walk by the way, when you lie down and when you rise up" (Deut. 6:7).

Why is this important? Because local churches help you preach the gospel to your children through many different experiences. Leverage your local church experience for the sake of the gospel. Make the most of those experiences. And, as you have probably already guessed, I hope to encourage you to make your local church the center of your family's schedule and priorities.

As a member of a local church, you are sitting on a golden opportunity. God has designed the church to help parents communicate about Him, His goodness, and the multifaceted powers of the gospel.

GOOD SHEPHERDS

If you are good shepherds, you will lead your flock to the greenest pastures and the purest waters. Like every good shepherd, you will work at it. You will take the lead. You will be out in front. You will think, pray, strategize, schedule, and act.

You are God's appointed tour guides for everlasting joy. By divine appointment, your job is to show your children wonders they've never seen before. If you are true Christians, you are opening doors. You are shining the light.

Do everything you can to make the local church sweet. Exult in her importance. Extol her beauty before your children. Why? So that your children will have an in-depth guided tour of the treasures of the gospel.

God has done a wonderful thing by giving you a family. It is likely the greatest earthly gift you will ever receive. By God's grace, you will take your family and build a beautiful little kingdom of love. So, how do you build that kingdom? I want to explain.

THE MOST PRESSING NEED

Nothing a family does is more important than hearing the gospel and meeting with God in the local church. The church of Jesus Christ meets your family at the junction of its most pressing needs. You need to know God, and you need to deal with your sin.

If you are parents, you passed on the defilements of original sin to your children. While salvation depends entirely upon God, He engages us. Now you must do all you can to work for their salvation as though it depends entirely upon you.

The Lord uses various means to pry the jaws of the devil and the effects of original sin off of your children and deliver them. The local church is central to His means. This is why you have a tremendous responsibility as parents to enfold your family in a local church. You need the help it provides. John Flavel speaks to the gravity of this responsibility:

> *"The most heartbreaking cry is that of the parent who has to honestly admit, 'My child is in hell and I did nothing to prevent it! My child is in hell and I helped him go there!'"*

He touches on how important this is:

> *"How few are converted in old age! A twig is brought to any form, but grown trees will not bow."*[1]

"My child is in hell..." how terrifying. Parents must ask themselves, "Did we do everything we could to prevent it? Did we do anything to speed him on his way to hell?" Good parents are not "hyper-Calvinists" who leave everything up to God, not lifting a finger to evangelize their children.

Can you see the opportunity before you? Do you have a vision for it? Are you poised for action? Are you willing to do what it takes? Why? So that everyone in your family gets a glimpse of the goodness of God. But, even more, that your children would hear the gospel and you would be able to say, "Today salvation has come to this house" (Luke 19:9).

This is why every family needs a local church family.

MISSING THE OPPORTUNITY

Don't be the person who missed the window of opportunity to cast visions of hope and joy in the gospel to your children. Don't be parents who wish you could turn back the clock and do it right on a second chance. There is no second chance. Someone once said that opportunity is like a train that starts to move. Once the doors close, the opportunity is gone. Raising children is like that. Your time with them moves faster than you think.

---

1 Flavel, J. (1985). *The Mystery of Providence* (p. 58). Edinburgh, Scotland: Banner of Truth.

This is why I am waving my arms and saying, "Don't miss this." As the sign says, "Nothing is more expensive than a missed opportunity." Do it for joy—everlasting joy.

TAKE THEM

Make it a wonderful adventure. Take them into the delights of hearing, singing, praying, learning, and responding. Don't passively take them. Take aim. Prepare them. Be a great tour guide. Usher them into His institution with happy zeal. It is nothing less than, "the body of Christ" (1 Cor. 12:27), "the city of the living God" (Heb. 12:22-24), the "flock" of God (John 10:16), "the church of the living God, the pillar and ground of the truth" (1 Tim. 3:15), the "bride" of Christ (2 Cor. 11:2; Eph. 5:25-27), the "temple of the living God" (2 Cor. 6:16), and the "people" of God (Lev. 26:12; Jer. 31:1).

A humdrum, robotic, cruise-control attitude in your local church won't serve your children well. When you take your children somewhere, it is really important that you know why you are taking them and what you want them to see.

There are at least two things that you need to do to accomplish this. First, you need to live a lifestyle all week long which makes the church a central part of your life. Second, when you go to church, you need to be a good tour guide.

Like everything else in life, children need your encouragement, inspiration, and engagement. They need interpretation. They need analysis. They need your help.

DISCUSSION

- What kind of tour guide have you been to your children in your local church?
- What kind of adventure would your children say they've been on in your involvement in the local church?

YOUR GOLDEN OPPORTUNITY

*"Look at the fields, for they are already white for harvest"
(John 4:35), and "The harvest truly is plentiful, but the
laborers are few. Therefore pray the Lord of the harvest
to send out laborers into His harvest" (Matt. 9:37-38).*

To be a competent tour guide for everlasting joy, you need to know that your family is sitting on a gold mine that is the local church. Your local church offers opportunities to speak of the multi-faceted beauties of the gospel of Jesus Christ. Each element of local church life presents varicolored ways to preach the gospel to your children.

A local church is like a diamond, with many facets reflecting light. God has allowed you to expose your family to these beauties—the beauties of the kingdom of God.

I want to mobilize you to walk your children through the treasure fields of the church of God. I want to help you to maximize the preaching of the gospel and the great deeds of God to your children through the gatherings of your local church. I want to show you how to explain the depths of the gospel of Jesus Christ to your children. This is how you increase joy in your family. It is a joy that comes through the saving knowledge of Jesus Christ. After all, you are a tour guide.

A GIFT

A local church is a wonderful gift to parents. It is divinely designed to assist you in the most important work you will ever do as a parent, which is to declare the glory of God to the next generation. Absolutely nothing is more important. It is your irreducible parental responsibility.

The gospel is rich and beautiful. Local churches have been perfectly configured by the Word of God to communicate its richness and beauty.

If you take full advantage of what is happening in your local church, you will be declaring the gospel over and over again, week by week, and year by year, through the diverse means that God has embedded in your local church.

Each element of local church life has been given to you as a good gift to help you "bring them up in the training and admonition of the Lord" (Eph. 6:4).

THE DANGER IN MISSING THE OPPORTUNITY

We are living in a period of history where the average church-going person has a poor understanding of God and the gospel. Biblical and theological illiteracy is rampant in churches. It is unconscionable. It is inexcusable given the opportunities that exist in local churches. Far too many have general thoughts about God. They can repeat a simple gospel message, but they are not clear on the multifaceted beauties of God's kingdom. They are ignorant of many major doctrinal categories and practical implications of the truth of God. The result is that they do not have much to pass on to the next generation.

TERMINAL IMMATURITY

One of the reasons that so many do not have a strong understanding of the Word of God, a biblical worldview, or the ability to think through the great movements of our society, is that families have not prioritized the local church. They have made the local church a sideline. They missed their opportunity. Therefore, the rich experiences that exist there were untapped.

This has been a disaster for the church, the family, and the culture. Shallow, insipid commitment to local churches is the root of much confusion, weakness, and many evils.

But you do not need to miss the opportunity if you, "Look at the fields, for they are already white for harvest."

DISCUSSION

- Have you underestimated the opportunities that exist in your local church to preach the gospel to your children?
- How have you been using local church life to teach the breadth of theological truth?

THE CHURCH
NEEDS STRONG FAMILIES

"But you must continue in the things which you have learned and been assured of, knowing from whom you have learned them, and that from childhood you have known the Holy Scriptures, which are able to make you wise for salvation through faith which is in Christ Jesus" (2 Tim. 3:14-15).

When God commanded Joshua to "be strong and very courageous," He also told him what he needed to do to be strong and courageous. He needed a laser beam focus on knowing and obeying the commands of God. In the same way, families are only as strong as their knowledge and their practices. If you want a strong family, you must do the things that strong families do. Further, the strength of your family will have a profound impact on the strength of your local church. This is why Thomas Manton declared in the introduction to the Westminster Confession of Faith:

"A family is the seminary of Church and State; and if children be not well principled there, all miscarrieth."[1]

You must grasp how important families are to the health of local churches. Families deliver both sinners and saints into the church. If your children are not instructed in the whole

---

1 Westminster Assembly (1643-1652). (2003). *Westminster Confession of Faith* (p. 9). Glasgow, Scotland: Free Presbyterian Publications.

counsel of God, the church will bear the burden. Please do not neglect your family. The health of a local church depends on how you govern your home.

Richard Baxter understood this very well:

> *"A holy, well-governed family is the preparation to a holy and well-governed church."*[2]

A family is like a feeder stream. A feeder stream is a small stream that flows into a larger one. A family is like that for the church. A family is small, but it feeds the larger church with people. The family is an ever-flowing stream, flowing into the church and the world at large.

The home life of Timothy is a powerful illustration of this. He was prepared for life by his mother and grandmother at home, using the Word of God. Paul writes of Timothy's home life saying, "When I call to remembrance the genuine faith that is in you, which dwelt first in your grandmother Lois and your mother Eunice, and I am persuaded is in you also" (2 Tim. 1:5).

Like Timothy's home, God designed your home to be a kind of nursery for the church. Every church member comes from a family. The individuals in a family are shaped by the beauty or the ugliness, the faithfulness or the rebellion experienced in that family. Think of the significance of the fact that the home fills the church with her members.

This is why I want you to understand that your home is like a feeder stream. This is why the health of a home is pivotal for the health of the church. God designed the home to be a discipleship community. It prepares children for the discipleship community of the church. This is how a home has such a profound impact on the health of a church.

---

2   *The Practical Works of Richard Baxter, Vol. 1: A Christian Directory.* (pp. 425-426). Ligonier, PA: Soli Deo Gloria Publications

Further, the home is a picture of the church. Here are three examples: First, the husband is the head of the wife in the same way Christ is head of the church. Second, wives submit to their own husbands, as to the Lord, picturing the submission that all people owe to God in the church. Third, the children in the home honor and obey their parents in the Lord, picturing the honor and obedience that all people owe to God in the church. This is why obedience to the commands of God for home life, prepare children for life in the church.

Unfortunately, the deficiencies and the "unpaid bills" of home life finally come due in local church life. On the other hand, the richness of the home, the "paid bills" add to the assets. This is why several of the older writers said that the family was the "seminary" of the church. They believed that if you neglected teaching in your family, the teaching in the church would not be very effective. Richard Baxter wrote:

> *"The life of religion, and the welfare and glory, both of the church and the state, depend much on family government and duty. If we suffer the neglect of this we shall undo all."*

Baxter continued:

> *"...what are we like to do ourselves to the reforming of a congregation, if all the work be cast on us alone, and masters of families neglect that necessary duty of their own by which they are bound to help us? If any good be begun by the ministry in any soul, a careless, prayerless, worldly family, is likely to stifle it, or very much hinder it..."*[3]

---

3   Baxter, R. (1799). *The Life of the Reverend Richard Baxter* (pp. 83-84). London, England: London Religious Tract Society.

Samuel Phillips said it this way:

> *"The church gives to home a sacred religious ministry, a spiritual calling, a divine mission".[4]*

Consider the profound impact Timothy's home had on his character and knowledge when he became a pastor. Paul wrote to him about continuing in the good things he learned at home:

> *"But you must continue in the things which you have learned and been assured of, knowing from whom you have learned them, and that from childhood you have known the Holy Scriptures, which are able to make you wise for salvation through faith which is in Christ Jesus. All Scripture is given by inspiration of God, and is profitable for doctrine, for reproof, for correction, for instruction in righteousness, that the man of God may be complete, thoroughly equipped for every good work"* *(2 Tim. 3:14-17).*

Here are eleven ways the family ought to be a nursery for the church:

First, it ought to be the place where sound doctrine is established:

> *"You shall teach them diligently to your children, and shall talk of them when you sit in your house, when you walk by the way, when you lie down, and when you rise up"* *(Deut. 6:7; Eph. 6:4).*

Second, it ought to be the place where wives are washed with the water of the Word, being beautified by their husbands through Scripture (Eph. 5:25-29).

---

4   Phillips, S. (1865). *The Christian Home: As It Is in the Sphere of Nature and the Church* (p. 35). Springfield, MA: Gurdon Bill.

Third, it ought to be the place where children are disciplined in the training and admonition of the Lord (Eph. 6:1-4).

Fourth, it ought to be the place where whole families hear the gospel and the lost turn to the grace of Christ (Eph. 6:4; Acts 10).

Fifth, it ought to be the place where godly seed is planted (via conversion) and grown:

> *"But did He not make them one, having a remnant of the Spirit? And why one? He seeks godly offspring" (Mal. 2:15).*

Sixth, it ought to be the place where the curse of God is held off:

> *"Behold, I will send you Elijah the prophet before the coming of the great and dreadful day of the Lord. And he will turn the hearts of the fathers to the children, and the hearts of the children to their fathers, lest I come and strike the earth with a curse" (Mal. 4:5-6).*

Seventh, it ought to be the place where husband and wife stand together as heirs of the grace of life:

> *"Husbands, likewise, dwell with them with understanding, giving honor to the wife, as to the weaker vessel, and as being heirs together of the grace of life, that your prayers may not be hindered" (1 Pet. 3:7).*

Eighth, it ought to be the place where iniquity is held back for generations to come:

> *"For I the Lord your God am a jealous God, visiting the iniquity of the fathers upon the children to the third and fourth generations of those who hate me, but showing mercy to thousands, to those who love Me and keep My commandments" (Ex. 20:5-6).*

Ninth, it ought to be the place of unity in marriage, where children learn that a house divided against itself cannot stand:

> *"So husbands ought to love their own wives as their own bodies; he who loves his wife loves himself. For no one ever hated his own flesh, but nourishes and cherishes it, just as the Lord does the church. For we are members of His body, of His flesh and of His bones. 'For this reason a man shall leave his father and mother and be joined to his wife, and the two shall become one flesh.' This is a great mystery, but I speak concerning Christ and the church. Nevertheless let each one of you in particular so love his own wife as himself, and let the wife see that she respects her husband" (Eph. 5:28-33).*

Tenth, it ought to give the church places to meet and where hospitality is practiced like the church which met in the house of Priscilla and Aquila (1 Cor. 16:19; 1 Pet. 4:9).

Eleventh, it ought to be the place where elders are prepared to be qualified:

> *"A bishop then must be blameless, the husband of one wife, temperate, sober-minded, of good behavior, hospitable, able to teach; not given to wine, not violent, not greedy for money, but gentle, not quarrelsome, not covetous; one who rules his own house well, having his children in submission with all reverence (for if a man does not know how to rule his own house, how will he take care of the church of God?)" (I Tim. 3:2-5).*

In these ways, YOUR home has a profound impact on the church for good or for ill. The church needs families that are functioning according to biblical order.

If you want strong churches, you must build strong households whether they are families, couples or singles. The

Bible makes it clear that the home needs the church and the church needs the home. They play dual and parallel roles. They cross-fertilize each other.

So, make your home a healthy feeder system, a beautiful nursery for the glory of God in your local church. As Baxter said, "If we suffer the neglect of this we shall undo all."[5]

DISCUSSION

- In what ways do you prioritize or de-prioritize the meetings of the church for the discipleship of your family?
- What kind of church members will your children be based on how you are preparing them?

---

5   Baxter, R. (1829). *The Reformed Pastor* (p. 158). Glasgow, Scotland: William Collins.

LOVE <u>THE</u> CHURCH

"LORD, I have loved the habitation of Your house, and the place where Your glory dwells" (Psalm 26:8).

The church is one of the places where God displays His glory. When Moses said to God, "Show me your glory," God showed him His goodness. This is what you ought to do as parents—show your children the goodness of the Lord. God, by His Spirit, is the only one who can finally reveal His glory to their hearts. However, you must take action to show it to them. By faith show it to them and then pray, "God, reveal your glory to my children."

We have already reviewed quite a few reasons why every family needs to be devoted to a local church. But how? In a word, "Zealously!" It should be the center of your lives. Why? Because Christ loves the church and the church is the center of His affectionate plans.

HOW IMPORTANT IS THE CHURCH?

God has always gathered His people for worship and discipleship in local assemblies. He starts this by rescuing His bride and calling sinners from the ends of the earth to gather and worship Him.

God is assembling multitudes to worship His Son for all eternity. He takes ownership of a people. He brings them into His house of worship to learn from Him and dine with Him. This is what the people of God do. They get together in local assemblies. In other words, He saves them, gathers them, and sanctifies them—together—not isolated from one another.

THE CENTER OF HISTORY

What happens in these local assemblies is the center of history. It is the storyline of the Bible—a people gathered for the glory of God. The history of the world is summed up in the triumphant rescue of sinners and giving them a new name and a new family. This is the church of Jesus Christ. This is why you need to make the center of history the center of your family life.

People today are not very discerning. They don't see the importance of things. When it comes to the church, they don't see it as central to their lives. It is, at best, a beneficial sideline.

Here is the big question I am driving at, "Are you zealously devoted to a local church?"

HOW DO YOU KNOW THE IMPORTANCE OF A THING?

Why would I assign such importance to your family's devotion to a local church? Well, how do you know the importance of anything? How would you accurately discern the relative value of one thing over another? You could value it by its approval rating. Or, you could rate it by its growth. Some folks rank it for how it contributes to your financial position, or how it enhances your ranking in society. But if you really want to know of the value of the church, look at who loves it, what is sacrificed for it, how long it lasts and how far-reaching its impact is.

Ultimately, you can tell what is important by what Christ says is important. In the case of the church, Jesus shed His precious blood for her (Acts 20:28). She is the most important institution that exists on the planet today.

Is the church important to you? If you are going to call yourself a Christian, then you ought to know if you love the things that God loves.

When I use the word "church" here, I am talking about a local church, not the universal church. This is the focus of the New Testament. Around 80% of the references to "church" or "ecclesia" in the New Testament are referring to local churches. The other 20% are referring to the universal church. Therefore, the main focus of the New Testament is on visible congregations of baptized believers—not the universal church.

Here is a good technical description of the local church:

> "The visible Church is the organized society of professing believers, in all ages and places, wherein the gospel is truly preached and the ordinances of Baptism and the Lord's Supper administered in true faith"[1]

This is referring to local churches which are pictured in the New Testament letters. For example, in Acts 2:42 we find this picture, "And they continued steadfastly in the apostles' doctrine and fellowship, in the breaking of bread, and in prayers."

In true local churches, you have people in community, meeting, eating, learning, singing, evangelizing, discipling, and loving one another.

Your family needs this kind of community. You were made for this kind of community.

HOW TO THINK ABOUT THE CHURCH

Think about the church the way Christ thinks of her:

> "Let this mind be in you which was also in Christ Jesus" (Phil. 2:5-7).

To have the mind of Christ toward the church, is to love her the way that Christ loves her and to behave the way Christ

---

1 (Question 105, *Baptist Catechism*, Benjamin Keach).

behaves toward her. John also urges us to have the mind of Christ, "He who says he abides in Him ought himself also to walk just as He walked" (1 John 2:6).

What does it look like to love the church? What does it look like to walk as He walked, within a local church? These are critical questions, since you as parents are the tour guides.

FOUR WAYS CHRIST LOVES HIS CHURCH

First, He gave Himself up for her (Eph. 5:24-30). He gave! His life was His own, and He laid down His life for His friends, shedding His own blood. Why did He do this? "… [T]hat He might sanctify and cleanse her with the washing of water by the word (Eph. 5:26). He desired to make her complete, to "present every man complete in Christ" (Col. 1:28). This means that His love is not theoretical. He loved His bride in spite of her deficiencies. He cares for her. He works for her purification. She comes to Him in rags and He gives her beautiful garments and a new name. He is always washing her.

What is His objective? "… [T]hat He might present her to Himself a glorious church, not having spot or wrinkle or any such thing, but that she should be holy and without blemish" (Eph. 5:27).

So, He gave Himself for His church.

Question: In what ways are you giving yourself to your local church?

Second, Christ personally identifies with the church. To illustrate, see the story of Saul persecuting the church. He was dragging both men and women out of their households and having them killed. Jesus says to him, "Why are you persecuting Me?" He is saying, "What you do to My church, is what you do to Me." This explains His intimate identification with the church. He is so closely identified with His church that there is no true local church or believer with which Christ is not personally identified (Acts 9:1-5).

Your family needs to understand that how they treat the church is how they are treating Christ Himself.

Question: In what ways are you identifying with or distancing yourself from your local church?

Third, He builds the church saying, "…on this rock I will build My church, and the gates of Hades shall not prevail against it" (Matt. 16:18). Jesus is building His church in hundreds of ways.

Question: In what ways are you building the church through your resources, talents, and spiritual gifts?

Fourth, He has zeal for His church, "Zeal for Your house has eaten me up" (Ps. 69:9, John 2:17). Christ has great passion for what He is building. This has to do with His attitude and feelings.

Question: Can you say that your attitude mirrors Christ's zealous love?

These are only four ways that Christ loved His church, but Scripture identifies many more. For example:

- He will never leave or forsake her (Heb. 13:5-6; Deut. 31:6,8).
- He sends her help and will not leave her an orphan (John 14:1-21).
- He comforts her (John 14:1-2).
- He sends prophets to speak to her (Jer. 29:19-20; Mark 12:1-12).
- He was poor yet made her rich (2 Cor. 8:9).
- He prays for her (John 17:9; Rom. 8:26).
- He draws her with lovingkindness (Jer. 31:3).

So, what about you? Do you have the mind of Christ for the church? Do His ways and desires shape *your* relationship with the local church? Do you want what you want, or what He wants? Are you building what He is building? Are you loving what He is loving?

The church is the only *eternal* institution Jesus established. Neither the family nor marriage are eternal (Luke 20:34-36). It is God's family that lasts for all eternity in heaven.

The church is extremely important to our Lord Jesus Christ, and it ought to be important to your family. Your family needs to hear the gospel preached. Your family needs to worship and sing. Your family needs the instruction, direction, correction, and protection only a local church can supply.

A DELIVERY SYSTEM

Churches deliver many things that your family needs to be healthy. Families need the routines, the ordinary means of grace, the relationships, and the conflicts that every local church provides. Yes, even the conflicts... You actually need the conflicts. You need to experience firsthand the disappointments and imperfections of a local church in order to be a healthy Christian. It is where you learn how to love people—just *unlike* you.

THE CENTER OF YOUR LIFE

As you are raising your family, make a local church the center of your life. Engage in the rhythmic experiences it offers. Love her like Christ loved her. Give yourself to her. Identify with her. Build her up and have zeal for her. To be like Christ is to love what He loves.

"Therefore be imitators of God as dear children. And walk in love, as Christ also has loved us and given Himself for us, an offering and a sacrifice to God for a sweet-smelling aroma" (Eph. 5:1-2).

I have observed the spiritual conditions of families over many years. Here is my conclusion. The families that keep the local church at the periphery of their lives are weaker. Something is missing. Something does not get connected. They miss a critical element of God's design for them. Growth in knowledge, mission, worship, maturity and longsuffering is stunted.

It is a very serious matter to be disengaged from Christ's bride. Loving the people in a local church is God's prep school and finishing school for love in every other area of life.

Since you have a family, you ought to nurture and cherish your children in such a way that you teach them to love what our Lord Jesus Christ loves. As tour guides of everlasting joy, you have an obligation to help them to say, "Lord, I have loved the habitation of Your house, and the place where Your glory dwells" (Ps. 26:8).

DISCUSSION

- Do you love your local church the way Christ loves her?
- Are you standing aloof from your local church because of your fear of being affected by its problems?

SHOW THEM <u>THE</u> TREASURES

"One thing have I desired of the Lord, that will I seek after, that I may dwell in the house of the Lord all the days of my life, to behold the beauty of the Lord and to inquire in His temple" (Ps. 27:4).

Take your children on a treasure hunt. But, in order to make it a great and profitable adventure, you need to know *what* the treasure is, and *where* it can be found. This puts you at an advantage.

This means that you already grasp what the church is, and what you are doing there. With this as a foundation, you will be able to better help your children find the treasure. If you know where it is, you can help them find it. This is the first step in leading them. Such knowledge will help you to engage them.

You are taking them to the promised land where the green pastures grow and still waters flow (Ps. 23). Help them taste the milk and honey. Open their "eyes to see wondrous things" (Ps. 119:18). Make it such a glorious experience that they say, "I was glad when they said unto me, let us go into the house of the Lord" (Ps. 122:1). Show them the beauty.

This is how David felt about the gatherings of God's people:

"One thing have I desired of the Lord, that will I seek after, that I may dwell in the house of the Lord all the days of my life, to behold the beauty of the Lord and to inquire in His temple" (Ps. 27:4).

It was the beauty he longed for. It is the beauty that your children need to see. You must marshal your whole soul and mind and strength to point them to it.

THE MOST IMPORTANT THINGS

Get excited for the most important institution on the planet. Put the central concern of God at the center of your life. And don't forget that your children are watching you! You are the one that sets the tone for how joyous your family will be on Sunday morning. Give them dozens of reasons to be joyful in it. Let them see your gratitude to God for a day set aside to worship. Show them the Lord's faithfulness. Help get their minds ready and excited about learning.

When you go to a local church, here is what you get:

- The most important institution—the church.
- The most important person—Christ.
- The most important book—the Bible.
- The most important people—the people of God.
- The most important activity—worship.
- The most important supper—the Lord's Supper.
- The most important delights—the means of grace.

Now, sit down with your children and explain each of the above points with them.

WHO IS PRESENT?

If these truths were not enough, Jesus promises to be personally present with His people. He is in our midst. He is walking among the "lampstands", the churches (Rev. 1:13-18). In Hebrews, we learn that Jesus is not ashamed to call us brethren and He is singing with His people in local churches.

He is saying, "Here am I and the children whom God has given Me" (Heb. 2:13 [See also, Matt. 18:20; Ex. 13:17-18; Ex. 25:8]). When we sing in our local churches, Jesus is singing with us, boasting in His joy to be with us. Jesus is, "God with us." He not only reveals Himself to us in His Word, but He is also present in His true children. He will never leave us nor forsake us.

LIFE-GIVING ACTIVITIES

Not only is our Lord Jesus present with us, but we are also brought into a diverse array of life-giving activities. Help your children get into it. Show them how wonderful it is to read the Word of God and hear the preaching. Help them savor the prayers and songs (1 Tim. 2:1-2,8; Col 3:16). Help them celebrate the fellowship, the Lord's Supper and Baptisms (Matt. 28:19; 1 Cor. 11:17-34).

Even if they are unconverted and unable to partake of the Lord's Supper, you can help them understand the purposes and the graphic imagery of the ordinance.

In other words, seize the Lord's Day. The day was "made for man" (Mark 2:27). It is "the day of delight." So, call it a delight and make it delightful (Isa. 58:13).

ENRICHING EXPERIENCES

Make sure your children understand the rich and diverse experiences God has designed. Help them enter into each part. They need your help. After all, they are children. Walk with them down the path to the living water.

GOD'S PLAN TO MEET WITH HIS PEOPLE

Teach your children that God has always gathered His people to worship Him. He has always brought His people together in consecrated spaces for holy moments. This is what God has always done.

This began with Adam and his family offering sacrifices. This was the first manifestation of gathering for worship. These holy gatherings are seen from Genesis to Revelation and continue in heaven for all eternity.

God has always gathered His people and He dwells with them when they meet. God is there, "The Lord is in His Holy Temple" (Hab. 2:20). Our Lord Jesus Christ is there, walking among His churches (Heb. 2:13; Rev. 1:13). We see this from the time of Adam and his family making sacrifices (Gen. 4:4-5; Heb. 11:4), to the Tabernacle, and on to the end of the Bible. God established places of worship to show His presence. The Tabernacle and the Temple were holy, inhabited by holy priests with holy garments and the families brought their sacrifices to worship. It was a family affair.

A CULTURE OF THANKSGIVING AND PRAISE

David testified to the happiness he felt going to the house of God (Ps. 122:1). He confessed this to the Lord, "Happy are those who dwell in Your house; they will still be praising You" (Ps. 84:4).

When we gather with God's people, who are they? They are His "special treasure" (Ex. 19:1-6), a "people for Himself," the "chosen," the "beloved," the "living stones," (Deut. 7:6; Isa. 41:8-9; 1 Pet. 2:5-10; Col. 3:12). It is a privilege to be with them. You have a responsibility before God to help your children experience the happiness of the moment and to bring your children into "His gates with thanksgiving" (Ps. 100:4).

God designed His church to be a wonderful collage of experiences and resources. There it is—a massively diverse resource. For you as parents, it is a wonderful gift from heaven, to be able to help your children have eyes to see the treasure and behold the beauty.

You shouldn't just *take* your children to church. Rather, *shepherd* them to see the beauty. But shepherd them with a plan—a plan to help them see the goodness of God. Show them what He offers to His children in your local church. Be a good tour guide.

Christians are to run the race with goals and objectives. We are not robotically or meaninglessly "beating the air." Rather, we aim our punches (1 Cor. 9:26). You dare not go to church without self-conscious, God-conscious intentionality.

Your children need your help. Don't make the church a place where you just show up. God gave His church to be a treasure trove of experiences and resources. Don't just *show up—power-up.*

Children love to be inspired. They are naturally wide-eyed when they are young. This is what is so much fun about raising children—they get excited about going places and doing things. So, be an inspiration machine. Take them on the most exciting, significant, and impactful treasure hunt ever. Perhaps all their life long they will desire "to behold the beauty of the Lord and to inquire in His temple."

DISCUSSION

- What are the specific ways you can power up, and make your children's experience more meaningful and impactful?
- What are you doing currently that minimizes the importance of the moments when you gather for worship on Sunday? In other words, what do you need to stop doing that minimizes the importance of the moment?

JOINED <u>AND</u> KNIT TOGETHER

"...[T]he whole body, joined and knit together by what every joint supplies" (Eph. 4:16).

None of us can survive without a diverse support system in the form of environments, ecosystems, food chains, economies, governments, seasons and many other things. God has created the whole world to be dependent. Your children need to experience a godly dependency in a local church. What do I mean? Let me illustrate using the reality of dependencies in an ecosystem.

Even small changes in ecosystems can cause trouble. I have cows. Cows need grass. Grass needs rain, nutrients, sun and seasons. But, the grass, in order to get healthier, needs the cows. The soil gets more fertile with cow manure. And... the cows need me and my fences to keep them focused on their mission. They are dependent creatures. They are dependent on me, and in some ways, the quality of the grass they eat is dependent on both of us.

SUPPORT SYSTEM

Your family is like that. Its health is dependent upon God-ordained support systems. Your family needs much more than your family can provide. Yes, you heard me right. Dad and mom, your children need more than your family to be healthy. God planned it that way, and He directs us on how to fill up what is lacking. Here is what church life provides.

SPIRITUAL BROTHERS AND SISTERS

How big is your family? God wants you to have a bigger one. The Bible makes it clear that you need spiritual brothers and sisters and fathers and mothers… these are necessary for spiritual growth. Look at the "one another's" listed in the Bible. There are over fifty of them and they describe how to get along with one another. They provide the best roadmaps for how to maintain healthy relationships anywhere. If you want to build a wonderful culture in church and home, these "one another's" are critical.

PASTORS

Further, you and your children need a mix of "pastors and teachers and evangelists…" for "the equipping of the saints for the work of the ministry" (Eph. 4:12-16). Your whole family needs men to teach them the Word of God in a way that you as parents cannot.

Your family needs the perspectives and personalities of a pastor who sees life differently than most people. Pastors actually see life differently. Trust me on that one. I know lots of pastors. Families need the exhortations and encouragements from a perspective that only pastors can provide.

Pastors are under divine obligation to make you uncomfortable with your life. They are under divine orders to exhort, correct and discipline you. God says you need such a thing. He makes it clear that ministers are required under their job description to "Give attention to reading, to exhortation, to doctrine" (I Tim. 4:13-16).

Further, you are required to submit to them, "Obey those who rule over you, and be submissive, for they watch out for your souls, as those who must give account. Let them do so with joy and not with grief, for that would be unprofitable for you" (Heb. 13:17). This is the consistent teaching of Scripture, "The ear that hears the rebukes of life will abide among the wise. He who disdains instruction despises his own soul, but he who heeds rebuke gets understanding" (Prov. 15:31-32). To submit to someone means that you don't always get your own way. You don't always agree. Your ministers might lead you in a direction you may not have chosen. This is good for the destruction of your pride. It grows humility. It increases honor toward your leaders and expands your trust in God.

DIVERSITY

Children need to rub shoulders with the rich, the poor, the experienced and the inexperienced, and the whole spectrum of humanity. They need the kind of diversity training that God provides in the church, where the hand cannot say to the foot, "I have no need of you" (1 Cor. 12:21).

PROBLEMS IN YOUR CHURCH? NO PROBLEM!

Everyone already knows that there is no perfect church. The London Baptist Confession of Faith acknowledges it, "The purest churches under heaven are subject to mixture and error".[1] But since we are not perfect either, having grace toward our imperfect brethren is a challenging matter. When you stay at one church for very long, you discover more and more imperfection. It can test your patience and your love.

In local churches, love is challenged. Imperfect people (sinners) mingle together and sometimes sparks fly. Disappointments happen. Objections are registered. Boredom might creep in. Distrust might grow. Leaders might fall.

---

1   1689 London Baptist Confession, 26.3

Your children need to experience all these things. But they will need the Word of God to show them how to make good out of it. Yes, they need the problems. Don't show them how to despise the problems. Don't teach them to run from them. Don't legitimize the feeling that leads them to say, "I'm done!" It is usually the devil's work when we give up on one another. In the same way beavers hate the sound of running water, the devil hates the sound of Christian unity:

> *"Satan always hates Christian fellowship; it is his policy to keep Christians apart. Anything which can divide saints from one another he delights in. He attaches far more importance to godly intercourse than we do. Since union is strength, he does his best to promote separation."*[2]

Families need to be in an environment where they get their feelings hurt. Why? This is how we learn to love one another. In fact, none of the commands in the Bible to "love one another," and "forgive one another," make any sense without offenses.

Love grows when something unlovely happens. When you are mistreated, you experience firsthand, the shortcomings of fellow church members and the leaders. It ought to remind us of the grace of God toward us as sinners who have offended God.

The offenses are good because they take us back to learning and re-learning how to practice the "one another's." These relational jewels called the "one another's," guide us through the relational minefields. They teach us how to respond in every possible church situation. Each one of them assumes

---

2   Spurgeon, C. (1865). *The Metropolitan Tabernacle Pulpit Sermons, Vol. XI* (p. 602). London, England: Passmore & Alabaster

sin patterns in our lives and how to live together in spite of them. These form the instruction manual for relationships in local church life.

Why do we need this? Why do we need one another?

"...[F]or the edifying of the body of Christ, till we all come to the unity of the faith and of the knowledge of the Son of God, to a perfect man, to the measure of the stature of the fullness of Christ; that we should no longer be children, tossed to and fro and carried about with every wind of doctrine, by the trickery of men, in the cunning craftiness of deceitful plotting" (Eph. 4:12-14).

DIVINELY DESIGNED ECOSYSTEM

God designed all of this to communicate the power of the gospel to our families. They help us to grow:

"...Speaking the truth in love, may grow up in all things into Him who is the head—Christ—from whom the whole body, joined and knit together by what every joint supplies, according to the effective working by which every part does its share, causes growth of the body for the edifying of itself in love" (Eph. 4:15-16).

This is why your family needs the influence of different people with different gifts. God created us to exist in the midst of a rich and diverse spiritual, divinely-designed ecosystem. The local church is part of that ecosystem.

This is just another reason your family needs the local church. God created His church to shepherd family members through a divinely ordained matrix of relationships and experiences and seasons. These diverse experiences are designed to refine you and show you His glory. This is a very important influence, because local churches launch one generation after another into the world to represent the kingdom God.

Samuel Rutherford speaks of it this way:

> *"The great Master Gardener, the Father of our Lord Jesus Christ, in a wonderful providence, with his own hand, planted me here, where by his grace, in this part of his vineyard, I grow; and here I will abide till the great Master of the vineyard think fit to transplant me."*[3]

We need a place to grow—a garden with soil. We are dependent. None of us, in ourselves, are adequate for the task. God has appointed the broad culture of His church to fill what is lacking. In a world of independence, we need to recover a biblically ordered interdependence. We need to be part of the ecosystem.

DO IT FOR JOY

All of this increases joy. Do it for your children. Show them how to preserve and deepen appreciation for their fellow travelers. The apostle Paul endured many difficult situations in local churches, yet he says:

> *"I thank my God upon every remembrance of you, always in every prayer of mine making request for you all with joy, for your fellowship in the gospel from the first day until now"* (Phil. 1:3-5).

The saints in Philippi were not super-Christians, yet he had them in his heart and they appeared in his prayers. He loved them.

---

3   Rutherford, S. (2007). *The Loveliness of Christ* (p. 1). Edinburgh, Scotland: Banner of Truth.

This is the joy that comes from participating in the body of Christ. It springs from knowing that God is in control, and that His grace working through obedience to His Word is sufficient in local church life. The fellowship of the saints is a gift. Make sure your children understand the joys, sorrows and obligations of being "joined and knit together by what every joint supplies" (Eph. 4:16).

DISCUSSION

- Have you inappropriately isolated your family from the members of your local body of Christ?
- Do you undervalue or underestimate the contributions of others in your local church?

FACE-TO-FACE RELATIONSHIPS

"And let us consider one another to stir up love and good works, not forsaking the assembling of ourselves together, as is the manner of some, but exhorting one another, and so much the more as you see the Day approaching" (Heb. 10:24-25).

God designed His church to be a face-to-face experience. In Acts 1:4 the saints are "assembled together." The biblical word, "church," (*ecclesia*) means "assembly" or "congregation" of people who gather together. The early church "gathered together" (Acts 2:42-47). The church, by definition, is a face-to-face affair. There is nothing remote about it. True church life cannot be experienced online.

Paul assumes that the church will meet together as evidenced by his statement, "When you come together in one place" (1 Cor. 11:20, 14:26). Luke documents these face-to-face meetings on the Lord's Day (Acts 20:7). The question is, does this match your behavior? Do you gather physically, in one place with the people of God, as they have for millennia? If you are not meeting face to face in a local church, then you are not a practicing Christian (unless you have some legitimate reason). You are practicing non-Christianity.

Hebrews 10:25 speaks to the necessity of meeting together. It is necessary because it is commanded. The author is correcting the people who are "forsaking." They are avoiding the gatherings because they don't prefer them and would rather do something else. Paul corrects that tendency by commanding them to draw near to one another.

TALKING HEAD CHRISTIANITY

Please do not mislead your children into thinking that Internet live-streaming church life is a real church. For those who think that live-streaming their church service is a true participation in church life, the way God designed it, think again. If you are live-streaming (unless you are ill or have a legitimate reason), you are only participating in a fraction of biblical church life. Of the activities outlined in Acts 2:42, you can only participate in a quarter of what God designed. But it's much worse than that. You cannot participate at all in the "one another's" that mark true Christian fellowship. The church is an institution that meets together, face to face. Don't settle for less. Your children need it!

If you have this kind of casual or online approach to your local church, don't be surprised if your children have the same. Make sure you understand this—if the church is a sideline for you, it will most likely be the same for your children. If your children think that online church is the same thing as going to church, you have misled them by your example. You have been a bad shepherd.

Many life-giving, life-shaping things happen in personal, face-to-face meetings that are impossible in online experiences. When the church meets together, everyone is exposed to dozens of beneficial forces. They all work on you in a different way—even the disappointments—by God's design.

LOVING THE SOCIAL LIFE

To help your children love the socio-spiritual life of the church, you as parents need to guard your own hearts first. Don't lose your love for the gatherings. Don't take them lightly. Don't be critical. It is just as important that you don't poison them. It is easy to poison children's attitudes toward the church. You can cause your children to become hyper-critical. Parents can forever poison their children against the local church and other Christians. They do it by criticizing the people, the preaching, the program, and the leaders of the church. It breeds a sense of distrust and dishonor that will never leave them.

If you face disappointments in your church, don't stop helping your children see the beauty. Don't make the meetings a sideline.

BUILD ANTICIPATION FOR THE JOYS OF FELLOWSHIP

Help your children anticipate the joys of fellowship. Simply driving to church can help prepare them. Get poised to help them out as you make the drive. Use it to get them ready for the action. The anticipations will roll around in their minds. They are passively getting prepared to meet people and experience the moments ahead. This is why Paul said of the Romans, "I long to see you" (Rom. 1:11). Hopefully, you all are saying in your hearts, "I was glad when they said unto me, let us go into the house of the Lord" (Ps. 122:1). The anticipation of being in the same room with your brothers and sisters changes the whole relational dynamic. When we meet in the same room, some things happen in our thinking and our feeling that shape us. It is multifaceted.

- When we arrive at church, we are met at the door by greeters. We are appreciated. In most churches, they greet you at the door like you are a king or a queen.
- Walking inside the church, you see smiles on faces.
- You may detect sorrow in an expression and compassion wells up within.
- You greet visitors and inquire about their lives.

- You realize that you missed seeing your brothers and sisters and you ask how they are doing.
- You are reminded that you have a big family—lots of brothers, sisters, mothers, fathers, grandmothers, grandfathers, uncles… you name it, the church has them in droves.
- You hear a member of the body—a spiritual relative—read the Word of God.
- You hear the sounds of the voices of brothers and sisters singing—my favorite sound.
- The whole congregation sings off the same page in unity, drawing us all together with one voice. Help your children see and feel how fantastic this is.

Help your children anticipate the God-given opportunities of the moments.

HOLY DIVERSITY

You are affected by the different kinds of people you meet. A local church offers you a holy diversity. For example, if you are seeing a new Christian or someone who is particularly godly or knowledgeable or holy, it affects you. You relate to them in a particular way.

You need all these different types of people in your lives. It is enriching. Help your children see and seize the opportunity to love and appreciate them. If you encounter someone who is living a worldly life, you recognize it and interact with that person thoughtfully and prayerfully. You relate with children differently than senior citizens. You relate to females differently compared to males. You are aware of the fatherless or motherless or childless in your big family.

Make sure your children understand how rich this is.

HOLY INTIMACY

This is totally different compared to seeing a talking head online. When we are in the same room, we sense that one person might be depressed or another might be happy. We are forced into uncomfortable situations being alongside a brother or sister who may have offended you. In local churches, there is usually someone we have a hard time relating with. Some people are socially awkward. Others are naturally distant or dispassionate and hard to talk to. God wants your children to have these experiences. Don't let them leave that church without seeing how beneficial this is to everyone.

Think of all the different kinds of people you find in a church. There are children and old people, singles and marrieds. All of these interactions are designed by God to supply something that is lacking. There is the subtle impact of sitting next to another person and hearing the sound of their voice.

SUB-CHRISTIAN

It is easy to see how the online "church" is substandard, but it is worse than that, it is sub-Christian. It simply does not compare with meeting together physically for true Christian fellowship. It is impossible to have a true Christian fellowship online. It is literally sub-Christian. It bears no reflection of the Christian in a true church.

Help your children experience the joys of church life. Spur them on to taste and see the beauties of meeting face to face. Lead them to appreciate the people and enjoy the diversity. Show them what the "one another's" look like. Open their eyes to the "gladness and sincerity of heart," as God designed. Do it to stimulate the "love and good works." Do it to increase their joy.

DISCUSSION

- What barriers can you identify that dampen the anticipation of the relational aspect of the local church?
- What are some things you can speak to your children about on the way to church to help them anticipate the meeting ahead?

THE DAY <u>OF</u> REST

"Remember the Sabbath day to keep it holy. Six days you shall labor and do all your work, but the seventh day is the Sabbath of the Lord your God. In it, you shall do no work: you, nor your son, nor your daughter, nor your male servant, nor your female servant, nor your cattle, nor your stranger who is within your gates. For in six days the Lord made the heavens and the earth, the sea, and all that is in them, and rested the seventh day. Therefore the Lord blessed the Sabbath day and hallowed it" (Ex. 20:8-11).

The Lord's Day is a family day. In the Ten Commandments, God appointed parents to usher their families into a day of rest on the Lord's Day. It is a holy day, different and more delightful than all the rest of the days of the week. As governors of households, the Lord commanded parents to make sure that everyone in their households, including their animals, experienced a day of rest. The jurisdictional responsibility for Sabbath-keeping rests explicitly on parents.

My objective in this chapter is to encourage you to make the Lord's Day a holy day of delightful spiritual rejuvenation for the whole family.

As we consider the Lord's Day in the life of a family, I will first take you through the primary arguments for keeping the Lord's Day. I want to challenge you to understand what the Word of God actually says about it.

What does the Lord's Day mean to you? The Lord's Day is many things to many people. Many simply ignore it as an outdated Old Testament relic. Some believe that the law of the Sabbath was abrogated and fulfilled by Jesus and is spiritual, not tied to a particular day. Others think of it as a new covenant option and not an obligation. For others, it is an old covenant bondage. You might think it is a day for relaxation or sports or doing whatever you want to do. You may think that any regulation on the day is an infringement on your freedom in Christ. Most evangelicals believe that observing the Lord's Day is the same as going to church for a couple of hours, and then you are free to do what you want.

CONFIRM YOUR POSITION ON THE LORD'S DAY

You ought to know with certainty what the Scriptures say and have a well-considered position on it. Why? There are at least two reasons. First, because you can't avoid taking a position on it. Each week you will have to decide how you will experience the Lord's Day. Depending on how long you live on this earth, God will give you hundreds, maybe thousands, of Sundays. Each one of them presents an opportunity to worship and adore Him on His Day or to do your own thing. It would be wise to have clarity on the biblical teaching and pass it on to your children. Second, if you embrace the observance of the Lord's Day the way the Bible prescribes, you will find yourself nearly alone in the evangelical landscape. Nearly the entirety of mainstream evangelicalism has quit celebrating the Lord's Day the way the Bible explains it.

WHAT DOES SCRIPTURE SAY?

Let me take you on a brief tour of what the Bible says about the Lord's Day. There are several passages of Scripture that give the heart of it. Each text provides insight into how you might increase the delights of family life.

AT CREATION, GENESIS 2:2-3

The first scriptural truth your children need to know is that at creation, long before God gave the law to Moses, God established a day of rest (Gen. 2:2-3). God Himself rested on the Sabbath as a pattern. Jesus bases his Sabbath observance on this fact: God rested (Mark 2:27). Further, the first day Adam and Eve spent on the earth was the first day of rest. But don't miss the detail in the narrative: He gave the Sabbath a special purpose and a name—the Sabbath day. He created light on the first day and animals and man on the sixth day. But, on the seventh day, He did something different. He created a day specifically allocated and separated (made holy) for rest. God rested. This is extremely significant. God Himself rested on the Sabbath as a pattern for humankind. To rest on the Sabbath is God-likeness.

BEFORE THE LAW, EXODUS 16:22-23

The people of God knew about and observed the law of the Sabbath before the Law was given on Mt. Sinai. The command to keep the Sabbath day is confirmed in Exodus 16:22-23, before the law of God was delivered in the form of the Ten Commandments.

THE TEN COMMANDMENTS, EXODUS 20:8-11

The second scriptural truth your children need to know is that in Exodus 20:8-11 and Deuteronomy 5:12-15, God reiterates the importance of God's day of rest, in the Fourth Commandment. Just like Jesus does in Mark 2, Moses lays the foundation of his argument upon God's resting at creation. This speaks of the duty of keeping this day "holy"—set apart from every other day. He assigns the family as the jurisdiction responsible for keeping it. God commands parents to ensure that everyone—including animals—in their households observe a day of rest. In the Law, the Ten Commandments, The Sabbath is a day of duty and holiness and rest—a day like no other.

THE PROPHETS, ISAIAH 58:13-14

The third scriptural truth your children need to know is that the prophets upheld the practice of keeping the Sabbath and spoke of the dangers of breaking it. In Isaiah 58, we learn that God ordered this day as a day of delight. Jeremiah made it clear that the reason for the Babylonian captivity is that Israel refused to keep the Sabbath for 490 years (God meted out a judgment of one year of captivity for every 7 years of neglect, for 70 years of captivity). In Jeremiah 17:19-27, we learn of God's judgment against Sabbath-breakers. In Ezekiel 20:12, we learn that it is a day to remember that God sanctifies His people. In Nehemiah 13:15-18, we see a historical example of the calamity that comes when God's people disregard the Sabbath and continue in their usual commercial activities. In the prophets, the Sabbath is a day of protection from judgment and a day of delight.

JESUS, MATTHEW 12:8 AND 24:20

The fourth scriptural truth your children need to know is that in the Gospels, Jesus upheld the Sabbath and corrected the Pharisees' legalistic and harmful misuse of it. Jesus supported this in Matthew 12:8, indicating that He Himself was the Lord of the Sabbath. In other words, He created it, defined it, observed it, and maintains it through His power as Lord. The religious leaders creatively encrusted it with harsh and unbiblical laws. Jesus consistently corrected their view by confronting them for adding ridiculous restrictions. Jesus does this by healing on the Sabbath and demonstrating that acts of mercy and necessity are lawful on the Sabbath. Jesus Himself keeps the Sabbath and He does not speak one word that discredits its observance. He shows us how to keep the Sabbath, not how to avoid it. Our Lord Jesus Christ speaks eleven times about the Sabbath, always correcting a wrong view. Further, Jesus assumes that Sabbath-keeping continues throughout the New Testament era, to the end of the world, "Pray that your flight might not be on the Sabbath day" (Matt. 24:20). In the Gospels, Jesus makes it clear that the Sabbath is *a day of healing and mercy and grace and the blessing of man*.

IT IS GOOD, MARK 2:27

The fifth scriptural truth your children need to know is "The sabbath was made for man" (Mark 2:27). These are the words of Jesus. He means that the Sabbath is a good thing for man. It is a benefit and a blessing. It is good for the body. You need a day of rest. It is good for the *mind* for your brain needs relief from grinding on the concerns of life. It is good for your *soul* for, "What shall it profit a man if he gains the whole world and loses his soul" (Mark 8:36)? It is good for your *heart* for, "It is good for the heart to be strengthened by grace" (Hebrews 13:9). It is good for your *conscience* for it is a day to confess that God is the sanctifier (Ezek. 20:12). It is good for your *family*, for the family needs time together with the saints. It is good for your *church,* for it makes it a happy church family. It is good for your *relationships* for it gathers spiritual brothers and sisters. Finally, it is good for your *nation*, for it blesses the people by preserving them from the wrath of God.

THE APOSTLES, ACTS 20:7

The sixth scriptural truth your children need to know is that the observance of the Sabbath continues in the ministry practices of the apostles (Acts 20:7; 1 Cor. 16:2). The apostles transformed the Jewish Sabbath into the Lord's Day—the day of the resurrection. The apostles changed its observance from Saturday to Sunday. The apostle Paul, and the churches he visited, observed the Lord's Day on Sunday. If you say that the Sabbath remains on Saturday, just realize that you are contradicting the apostles. You are overturning the fixed practice of the church ever since.

Be wary of using Colossians 2:16 to abolish the Lord's Day. Paul is referring to "festival or a new moon or sabbaths." Paul is not extinguishing the Sabbath in this text. Instead, the word Paul uses for "sabbaths," often refers to the Jewish feasts of the ceremonial law. Be careful that you don't throw out the entire testimony of Scripture over one verse, which could mean that the feasts of the ceremonial law have expired, being fulfilled by Christ, and are no more necessary than the sacrifices of bulls and goats in the temple in Jerusalem.

IT REMAINS, HEBREWS 4:1–11

The seventh scriptural truth your children need to know is that in the letter to the Hebrews, God proclaims that the essence of the Sabbath observance is "rest" because there is rest in the atoning sacrifice of Jesus Christ. Modern churches often use this passage of Scripture to reject the celebration of the Lord's Day because Jesus fulfilled it. Is this what Hebrews 4 means? The text does not necessitate this interpretation any more than the seventh commandment (you shall not commit adultery) is abrogated because Jesus "fulfilled it." Instead, it proclaims that the physical day in the Old Testament pictured rest in Jesus Christ. Knowing our Lord Jesus is to know rest, but the Sabbath day and the rest we receive from it, "remains." Hebrews uses explicit language proving the perpetuity of the Sabbath, "the promise remains," and "let us be diligent to enter that rest" (Heb. 4:1-11).

THERE ARE TEN COMMANDMENTS

The eighth scriptural truth your children need to know is that there are ten, not nine, commandments. One thing is clear: there are ten commandments in the moral law of God. They were written in stone on Mt. Sinai. There is no indication in the Bible that there are only nine commandments for today. You need to decide if you *actually* believe that there are only nine commandments. If you think there are only nine, why not only six commandments, or two? Is that a legitimate way to approach the Ten Commandments?

IS WORK ABROGATED?

In Exodus and Deuteronomy, the rhythm of work and rest are packaged together. Working six days and resting one day is part of a total weekly plan that God ordained for mankind. If you believe you are not obligated to keep the Lord's Day, then why would you think you are obligated to work? These two things are mingled in the command "work six days," and "remember the Sabbath day."

ARE THE OTHER COMMANDMENTS ABROGATED?

If you believe that you are not obligated to keep the Lord's Day, which is mandated in the moral law of God, then why are you obligated to refrain from theft and adultery and idolatry?

When you minimize the importance of the Lord's Day, you minimize basic elements of historic Christianity. These elements are communicated in some of the great and enduring confessions and catechisms of the faith, such as the 1689 London Baptist Confession and the Westminster Confession of Faith.

Even the enemies of Christianity understand that to *observe* the Lord's Day of rest is to *preserve* Christianity. During the French Revolution, the revolutionaries thought they could destroy Christianity by destroying the Sabbath. So, in a failed attempt to wipe out Christianity, the state mandated a ten-day work week. They threw out the seven-day week that the Sabbath rested upon and established the "Revolutionary Calendar." They did it for twelve years. No Sundays! No weekends for twelve years! It was a disaster. The ten-day work week ran totally out of kilter with the sun, moon, and stars and the structure of the solar system. It fouled up everybody's life. They finally went back to a seven-day week when Napoleon took over.

Here is the lesson from the French Revolution: don't mess with God's rhythms or His day. Why? By ignoring the day of *satisfaction and rest,* you deprive yourself of the delight God planned for you.

God commands you as parents to make sure your family experiences a day of rest. God created it to be a holy and most special day. He delivered this command for our good, for our rest and our delight.

So, what about you? What is your position? Here is Robert Murray M'Cheyne's position. It reflects the testimony of the Sabbath at creation, in the law, in the prophets, by the Lord Jesus, by the apostles, and the practice of the early church.

"It is a type of heaven when a believer lays aside his pen or loom, brushes aside his worldly cares, leaving them behind him with his weekday clothes, and comes up to the house of God. It is like the morning of the resurrection, the day when we shall come out of great tribulation into the presence of God and the [L]amb when the believer sits under the preached Word and hears the voice of the Shepherd leading and feeding his soul..."[1]

Parents, remember the Sabbath day to keep it holy. Make sure that everyone in your household knows the blessedness of delightful rest. Remember to explain to them all the reasons you are doing such a thing.

DISCUSSION

- Can you prove, using the Scriptures alone, the necessity of the duty to keep the Lord's Day?
- What do these passages of Scripture mean and what do you think of them?

NOTE

For clearly stated proofs of the Sabbath, the duties of the Sabbath and how to interpret the moral and ceremonial law of God, see the Baptist Confession of 1689 chapter 22, "Of Religious Worship and the Sabbath Day," and chapter 19 "On the Law of God," and chapter 21 "Of Religious Liberty and Liberty of Conscience."

---

1   Bonar, A.A. (1995). *Memoir and Remains of Robert Murray M'Cheyne* (596). Edinburgh, Scotland: Banner of Truth.

DELIGHTFUL CELEBRATION

"Then you shall delight yourself in the Lord, and I will cause you to ride on the high hills of the earth, and feed you with the heritage of Jacob, your father. The mouth of the Lord has spoken" (Isa. 58:14).

In the previous chapter I wanted to communicate a biblical case that God desires for you to keep His rhythms for your life and to fill your family with delight (Isa. 58:13-14; Ps. 16:11; Ps. 1:1-6). It is a requirement. This is why He prescribes a day of delight for the family—The Lord's Day—Sunday. Jesus declared that the day was "made for man," not the man for the day. In other words, the day is a benefit and a blessing to man, not a burden. Now, I would like to talk to you about *how* to celebrate the Lord's Day.

The critical factor in *how* to celebrate begins in your mind. How you *think* about the day makes all the difference. God promises to increase your delight if you change your mind about it and think of it as a delight. This starts by *calling* it a delight.

"Then you shall delight yourself in the Lord, and I will cause you to ride on the high hills of the earth, and feed you with the heritage of Jacob, your father" (Isa. 58:14).

Don't deprive your children of the opportunity for blessings God has promised. In doing so, you are setting a course for an entire life of delighting in the Lord.

BORING?

You parents can make the Lord's Day a bore. You can make it an offense by the way you plan and order the day. Making children sit like statues on the Lord's Day is not the way to make it a day of delight. It exasperates them. It deprives them of profitable activity. It is one way you can cause your children to sin. And don't forget, you are commanded by God to keep from exasperating your children (Eph. 6:1-4).

A HAPPY AND HOLY DAY

By trusting in the grace of Christ and relying on His Spirit and His Word, you are under divine obligation to create a day that is holy and happy. You need to pray for wisdom and creativity. You parents ought to put your heads together and work thoughtfully to help your children experience the Lord's Day as the best day of the week.

If your children are bored, it is most likely your fault. You have some adjustments to make. Don't let it continue. You need to keep considering how to make it the best day of the week. Don't blame the boredom on the day. And, don't break the Lord's Day just because your children aren't enjoying it. Instead, consider again how you can make it the most helpful, exciting, encouraging, and unique day of the week. This is your job as parents. It is a tough job, but somebody has to do it.

The Scriptures are clear. The jurisdictional responsibility for keeping the Lord's Day, and making it a delight, falls directly on the parents in a family (Ex. 20:8-11; Deut. 5:12-15). If your Sundays are not a delight, the way God describes it in His Word, then look to yourself and identify the flaws in your leadership. God passed the jurisdictional responsibility to you as parents for ensuring your family rests and delights in the Lord. You have an obligation to make it work.

RESTRICTIONS?

What are the specific biblical restrictions prescribed for the Lord's Day? There are only a few restrictions mentioned in the Bible: cease from work, cease from regular activity, cease idle talk, and cease from doing your own thing. That's it. God gives broad principles that apply broadly (Ex. 20:8-11; Deut. 5:12-15; Isa. 58:13-14).

Let's make it simple: Through these commands, God is teaching us to eliminate the things that distract us from glorying in our Redeemer and finding our joy in His ways, His Words, and His work. We don't need specific laws to tell us when this is happening and when it's not. We usually know when we drift. We have a conscience. The Holy Spirit did not make us total idiots who need a rule for everything. The general guidelines under the illuminating ministry of the Holy Spirit and the conscience should be enough to train us to make the Lord's Day holy. Everyone knows when they are pursuing irrelevant or silly things. Everyone knows when they are not entering "into His gates with thanksgiving and into His courts with praise" (Ps. 100:4).

Remember, the Scriptures call for an entire day, not a half day. We have the privilege of getting to do things that are different from the rest of the days of the week. What's the big difference? I'll summarize it in two words: delightful celebration.

DELIGHTFUL CELEBRATION

Isaiah 58:13-14 gives new covenant believers some practical thoughts for celebrating the day of worship. Isaiah explains some of the most useful reasons to be thoughtful about the Lord's Day. It is a day to turn to the most pleasurable activities for the soul. Isaiah instructs us on how to experience the delight God has desired in His holy day:

83

1. Regard the Sabbath as a delight, "and call the Sabbath a delight." In other words, how you think about it changes everything about it. Regard it as a joy, not a drudgery. Call it that! Call the Sabbath a delight.

2. Give special honor to the day as we are to call it, "the holy day of the Lord honorable." In other words, make it more special than any other ordinary day. Call it a special day.

3. Set your heart to honor God to fulfill His desire, "and shall honor Him." In other words, proactively name the day, the day to honor Him.

4. Turn away from your preferences to what God prefers, "not doing your ways." In other words, do the things that God says are a blessing.

5. Turn away from seeking your own pleasure, and turn to the pleasures of God, "nor finding your own pleasure." In other words, turn off and shut down trivial pleasures.

6. Turn away from speaking idle words, "Nor speaking your own words." Be less trivial in your speech. Consider how you might talk about the really important things. For example, look to the Word of God and speak the Word of God as much as the Lord gives you strength, "Let the words of my mouth and the meditations of my heart be pleasing in Your sight" (Ps. 19:14).

HOW DO YOU HELP YOUR CHILDREN CELEBRATE SUCH A DAY?

Examine

To help your children fully enter into the joys of the Lord, you need to be certain types of people. You, as parents, must be born of God's Spirit with His Law written on your heart (Jer. 31:31-34). Examine yourselves to see if you are real children of God.

Delight

You must delight in the Lord's Day yourself. Your disposition of delight in the Lord's Day is the most powerful apologetic. Show your enjoyment by preparing your family for it. When you are excited about something, it is infectious. Say to them what David said:

> *"I was glad when they said unto me, let us go into the house of the Lord" (Ps. 122:1).*

Show your delight by snapping into action. Help them build excitement for the day. Teach them the applications of the sermon and the Scriptures you encountered at church that day. Show your enjoyment by glorying in the songs of the day. Demonstrate your pleasure by giving thanks for the preaching and help them understand it.

Prepare

Prepare the ground for the Lord's Day on Saturday. The Jews observed, "the day of preparation." This was the day before the Sabbath. Families prepared meals and whatever was necessary to make the Sabbath a day of rest.

Plan

Parents need to plan the day for delight. This obligates you, parents, to trust Christ to help you preserve that delight by the power of the Holy Spirit. It is unprofitable to have an unplanned day of just sitting and doing nothing. After the church services, continue to rejoice in the Lord.

Here are eleven ways (and there are many more) that families can continue the day of delight at church:

1. Review the sermon in the afternoon.
2. Take a walk and rejoice in the glory of God's work in creation.
3. Sing psalms, hymns, and spiritual songs together.

4. Pray together.
5. Memorize Scripture together.
6. Listen to a sermon.
7. Read *The Pilgrim's Progress* or listen to it on audio.
8. Read a biblically-sound book about church history, or a Christian biography.
9. Write down your thoughts from your time at church.
10. Have little ones draw pictures about the sermon.
11. Take time to sit and talk about the week before and the week ahead.

You have three critical responsibilities regarding the Lord's Day:

First, by faith in Christ, through works of love, take responsibility for leading your family to observe the day.

Second, you must desire to experience the delightful blessings of the Lord's Day.

Third, you must pray earnestly for your children, prepare them for worship, and demonstrate for them the delights of celebrating the resurrection of our Lord Jesus Christ and the blessings of His kingdom.

EXCUSES

There are many reasons that we can give to avoid celebrating with the saints on any given Lord's Day. Having little children can cause families to devalue the Lord's Day. When you are midstream in the season of life when you have lots of little children, worrying can cause temptation. Because it is difficult, you might try to justify being absent from your local church. Young mothers with many small children are often tired at the end of the week. It can be tempting to think, "Well, it's supposed to be a day of rest, and the only way we're going to get any rest is by staying home."

When this happens, remember this: resting in the Lord doesn't mean leisure. This day is not primarily one of physical rest or doing nothing. While there can be elements of this, our first aim is to make it a completely different kind of day of spiritual rest. We rest from our usual work in order to be fed and encouraged by finding spiritual rest in Christ and His church.

We might think physical rest is what we need. Pampering ourselves is not normally what we need. When we commune with the Lord and honor His commands, He will provide His rest for us. He will make sure that you will be blessed. That includes stamina and strength to continue in the work that is coming on Monday.

Delighting in the Lord's Day sets your family on a journey of delight every week of their lives. Thomas Watson explains:

"When the falling dust of the world has clogged the wheels of our affections, that they can scarce move towards God, the Sabbath comes, and oils the wheels of our affections and they move swiftly on. God has appointed the Sabbath for this end."[1]

The Lord's Day was designed to be like oil, water, and sweetness of delight for the whole family. You as parents are charged by God to make it happen. Guide them to ride on the *"high hills of the earth."*

DISCUSSION

- How are you keeping the Lord's Day the way the Lord prescribes?
- How are you trusting the Lord to make His Day the best day of the week?

1 Watson, T. (1965). *The Ten Commandments* (pp. 94-95). Guildford, England: Billings and Sons, Ltd.

THE FAMILY TOGETHER <u>IN</u> CHURCH

"... [W]hen all Israel comes to appear before the LORD your God in the place which He chooses, you shall read this law before all Israel in their hearing. Gather the people together, men and women and little ones, and the stranger who is within your gates, that they may hear and that they may learn to fear the LORD your God and carefully observe all the words of this law, and that their children, who have not known it, may hear and learn to fear the LORD your God as long as you live in the land which you cross the Jordan to possess" (Deut. 31:11-13).

The pattern of Scripture shows families gathering together for worship and discipleship. This is the reason you should keep your children with you when you worship in the local church. The Bible shows many scenes where families were together for worship, prayer and discipleship. It is nearly impossible to find age-segregated gatherings for worship and fellowship in the Bible. This is the reason you should consider opportunities to keep your children with you when you worship in the local church.

However, we live in a culture that almost always separates families into age-graded subgroups. Did this come about because we were thinking biblically about it? Not really.

A BIG VISION OF GOD

Children need to be inspired with a big vision of the greatness of God. How do you give it to them? You give it to them by showing them the majesty of God, the truth of God, the seriousness of sin, the power of the gospel and the relief of redemption. This is the heart and soul of local church meetings. Or, at least it should be.

All this to say, one of the indispensable ways parents do this is by bringing them to participate in the rich and various experiences of the meetings of the church.

WHY DO WE SEGREGATE THE GENERATIONS?

Here is the short history. The modern pattern of separating families (and systematic age segregation) in the church was copied from the public education system. The church fell in love with this practice in the 1850's with the rise of public education under the guidance of ungodly educational philosophers such as Horace Mann and John Dewey. The movement grew and it picked up steam all over the world. Then, in the 1950's, in America, we saw the rise of a new and innovative obsession—youth culture and its offspring—youth ministries. It gave birth to youth rallies, youth groups, youth pastors, and a version of segmentation of the church that no one had ever seen before. Everything in the church became age-segregated. These popular practices spread all over the world.

But if all we followed was the Bible, would we do it this way in the church? What does the Bible say?

EXAMPLES OF FAMILIES WORSHIPING TOGETHER

Here are a few examples of families worshiping together, celebrating or engaging in discipleship in the Bible. Notice the many beneficial things the families were engaged in during these gatherings—worship, adoration, confession, repentance, prayer, and reading.

Passover

In Exodus 12:1-28, we learn that whole families celebrated deliverance from bondage in Egypt at the Passover feast. This was a seven-day family celebration. Moses says, "Pick out and take lambs for yourselves according to your families" (Ex. 12:21). It was designed for the children to learn about bondage and redemption in Egypt, "And it shall be, when your children say to you, 'What do you mean by this service'?" (Ex. 12:26).

Tabernacle

In Leviticus, the whole family was commanded to bring sacrifices to the tabernacle for atonement for sin. The sacrificial system was a family affair. Sacrifices had been brought to the Lord by families since Cain and Abel. In the first chapter of Leviticus, we encounter very specific instructions for both people and priests. Let us not forget that it was families who brought their sacrifices. These sacrifices were acknowledgments of sin in the families. There were five sacrifices specified. First, the burnt offering for atonement (1:1-17). Second, grain offering for personal consecration (2:1-16). Third, peace offering for reconciliation with God (3:1-17). Fourth, sin offering for propitiation for unintentional sins (4:1-5:1). Fifth, trespass offering for repentance (5:14–6:7). The whole family was involved at some level.

Sabbath Feasts

In Deuteronomy 12, Moses explains how parents must bring their families to "the place where the Lord your God chooses" out of all your "tribes," to rejoice in God. The families (tribes) are commanded to bring their offerings to these places the Lord chooses, and they are to eat together and rejoice together to worship God as families, "And you shall rejoice before the

Lord your God, you and your sons and your daughters, your male and female servants and the Levite who is in your gates" (Deut. 12:11-12). This activity is specifically not to happen in the home but in the place the Lord chooses (Deut. 12:17-18). This forms the consistent pattern of the worship of God in the Bible.

Outdoor Discipleship Experiences

In Deuteronomy 27:11-26, we see all the families of Israel gathered on Mt. Ebal and Mt. Gerezim to recount the blessings of obedience and the curses of disobedience. They shouted the curses and blessings to one another, antiphonally from the tops of these two mountains. Many of the blessings and the curses have to do with family life.

In Deuteronomy 12:6-7, we find families commanded to worship God, to rejoice together at the feasts and to bring their tithe money, turn it into cash and "rejoice with your household."

Reading the Law

In the days of Moses, God commanded families, including the "little ones" to come together every seven years to hear the reading of the Law of God (Deut. 31:12-13). This was practiced for hundreds of years in Israel.

In Joshua 8:35, we learn that Joshua read all the words of the Law, to whole families on Mount Ebal (Josh. 8:35).

In Nehemiah 8:1-2, everyone gathered to hear the reading of the Law of God. Who was present? Everyone, including the little ones, except those who "could not understand," most likely because half the children only knew the language of Ashdod, not the language of the Hebrew Bible (Neh. 13:24).

Rejoicing After Revival

In Nehemiah 12:43, we read the story of reformation and rejoicing, and women and children included in the public gatherings.

Worship and Prayer on Threat of Attack

In 2 Chronicles 20:13, children and wives were prayerfully present in time of danger of invasion. The children were included in singing and prayer in the face of battle. This must have left an unforgettable impression on their young minds.

In the Temple

In 2 Chronicles 31:18, the families were before God in the temple to sanctify themselves.

In Seasons of Repentance

Joel 2:15-16 describes a time of repentance where whole families came, even brides and bridegrooms on their wedding day.

New Testament Examples

In the New Testament, we see the same pattern of families involved together in the life of the gathered church. There is no explicitly biblical evidence that the church was ever separated by age.

Jesus and the Little Children

In Matthew 18:2-3, Jesus called a little child to hear Him, and used him to illustrate the doctrine of salvation, "Unless you are converted and become as little children, you will by no means enter the kingdom of heaven." On another occasion, recorded in Matthew 19:13-15, the disciples rebuked children who drew near to Him. Then, Jesus rebuked the disciples for restraining the children.

The Temple of Jerusalem

In Matthew 21:15-16, we learn that children were in the temple and they were crying out. But, the Pharisees did not approve of this. The children cried out, "Hosanna to the Son of David!" But the Pharisees "were indignant and said to Him, 'Do You hear what these are saying?'" Jesus publicly correcting them, "…said to them, 'Yes. Have you never read, "Out of the mouth of babes and nursing infants You have perfected praise"?'" It seemed normal to Jesus that the children were in the temple.

Jesus Teaching the Multitudes

In Matthew 14:21, when Jesus fed 5,000 men, there were women and children present also, "Now those who had eaten were about five thousand men, besides women and children." In the following chapter, the same conditions existed when He fed 4,000 men (Matt. 15:38). Most interpreters suggest that Jesus was preaching to 15,000-25,000 people of different ages and genders during each of these events.

Prayer Times

In Acts 21:5, we find the children joining their parents in prayer on the beach, "…We departed and went on our way; and they all accompanied us, with wives and children, till we were out of the city. And we knelt down on the shore and prayed."

Local Church Meetings

In Ephesians 6:1-4, the setting is the gathered church. The apostle Paul directly addresses the children in the assembly, "Children obey your parents in the Lord." These are the children who are sitting in the meeting of the Ephesian church who are hearing the letter read. Paul uses a Greek grammatical form called the "vocative of direct address."

He is directly addressing the children in the meeting of the church. It is clear that children were present in the meetings of the early churches. Paul assumes the children are present for the reading of his letter to the Ephesians.

In his commentary on Ephesians, William Hendricksen explains it this way:

> *"Were Paul to be present with us today he would be shocked at the spectacle of children attending the Sunday School and then going home just before the regular worship service. He has a word addressed directly and specifically to the children."*[1]

The meetings included young boys like Eutychus (probably between 7 and 14 years old) who left the meeting after midnight by falling out a window. He was overcome with sleepiness during a long Pauline preaching session, nodded off and rolled off the window's ledge (Acts 20:7-12).

We need to understand that the meetings in the early church included babies who were cutting teeth, eight-year-old boys who were wired for movement, and budding teenagers. The children were not in age-graded Sunday schools instead of the meetings of the church. They were taught side by side with adults in the meetings of the church.

On the flip side, are there explicit biblical examples or commands or principles that lead us to segregate the church by age? No! Not in the Bible. You will have to go somewhere else to find it. You cannot make an explicit case for age segregation by using the Bible. You have to go to some other source.

---

1   William Hendricksen, *Galatians and Ephesians* (Grand Rapids: Baker, 1979) pg. 258.

TEACHING ON THEIR LEVEL

Now the big question is, "Don't children need to be taught on their level?" Here is my answer: in some contexts, yes it seems to make sense. However, to deduce that this is reason enough to implement and maintain fragmentation of the gathered church for worship suggests a practice totally foreign to the witness of the Scriptures. We do not have record of it in the Bible. Does the Bible ever tell us that children need to be taught on their level in the church? If we are going to fragment the worship of God in the church by learning levels, I believe we need to have a clear biblical warrant for it. To my knowledge, there is no biblical warrant. I believe that whatever is done in the church of Jesus Christ must have biblical warrant.

Could it be that God has so arranged His church so that children would increase in their knowledge as they naturally grow up hearing the preaching and teaching of His Word? They grow in spiritual maturity as their cognitive abilities rise.

God has given, in His Word, all the principles and practices we need to teach our children in His church. It seems that children grow through a progressive acquisition of wisdom and knowledge over time, through the normal gatherings of a local church. The children understand a little when they are little and a lot when they are big. That's God's plan. I'm content to let that happen organically over time as they receive the Word of God, with the help of their parents, week by week.

There is no indication from Scripture that children were removed from the meetings designed for preaching, Scripture reading, prayer, and worship. That's the Christian way. Go and do the same. Keep your children with you for worship and discipleship.

DISCUSSION

- In your own words, describe the biblical testimony for keeping your children with you in church.
- If you are reluctant to keep your children with you in church, what is holding you back?

KEEPING CHILDREN
<u>IN</u> WORSHIP SERVICES

"Children, obey your parents in all things for this is well pleasing to the Lord." (Col. 3:20)

"Children, obey your parents in the Lord, for this is right. 'Honor your father and mother,' which is the first commandment with promise: 'that it may be well with you and you may live long on the earth'" (Eph. 6:1-3; See also Ex. 20:12; Prov. 25:28).

L et's talk about helping your children observe the glory of Jesus Christ in all of its attributes, deeds and instructions. God gives you many opportunities to show your children His majesty and set them up for success at the same time. Local church life is one of them. Keeping children of all ages with you in church services can be tough sledding. It creates interesting situations—sometimes exasperating situations. It can be embarrassing and distracting. Having your little children with you can feel like *you* just missed *half* the sermon. You start thinking that *your children* missed the *whole* sermon. The Lord's Supper tray can be precarious in little hands. It is easy to get frustrated.

Keeping your children with you often exposes defiant hearts, right in front of God and everybody. Sometimes sin in the hearts of the parents is exposed. These experiences reveal things that need to be addressed before the Lord. The exposure is good. Hopefully, repentance and sanctification ensue.

99

In the first few years of a child's life, parents often find themselves in a constant battle to stay on top of things. It seems it will never end. So, why not just hide them in the nursery for a while? You get the idea.

Here are some practical suggestions to help you keep your children with you in the church service.

PREPARE THEM

A church worship service may stretch out to 90 minutes—like most movies. However, church services are not like movies. Church services for the glory of God, properly experienced, require preparation. So, you need to talk to your children about it. Help them see how the time will be allocated. Deliberate preparation is very helpful to children who sit in church services.

ROLE PLAY

It is very helpful to role play the service situations. This is when you make sure the rules are clearly communicated. Here are some of the objectives we tried to uphold (though imperfectly) in the Brown household:

- Sit still
- Look at the speaker
- Listen to the speaker
- Sing wholeheartedly
- Show respect for other worshippers
- Don't turn around
- Don't make faces at other people

Some of my children (now that they have their own children) have their little ones fold their hands together during worship. At the beginning, when they are little, they might hold the child's hands together to keep them from flying apart. It works very well, and it helps them to keep focused, keep from bugging siblings next to them, and from playing with things.

FAMILY WORSHIP TRIAL RUNS

You should have a time daily when your family gathers around Scripture. Do it from the time they are babies. The best way to prepare your children for church meetings, is to maintain daily worship in your home. This is the training time where all of the disciplines of the meeting of the church are engaged in, within the privacy of your own home. Divide your time together with singing, Scripture reading, memorization and prayer. In other words, duplicate some of the familiar elements of a church service. You might even consider listening to a recorded sermon. This way the child is hearing someone else's voice, just like they do in the worship service.

The church service should not be your primary training ground. Rather, family worship in the privacy of your own home should be where your primary training takes place.

IT'S A SET-UP

What's this all about? You are setting them up to succeed! I cannot emphasize this enough. Well-ordered family worship is indispensable for preparing them for Sunday. If they cannot learn to sit still and listen in the privacy of your own home without distractions, YOU are setting them up for failure and yourself for frustration on Sunday morning. Orderly home life is the key to orderly church life.

ESTABLISH BIBLICAL STANDARDS OF BEHAVIOR

The fifth commandment requires children to obey parents (the first time). This is the baseline for all child training. It forms the structure of honor that is necessary for a child's success in life (Eph. 6:1-4). You need to wisely deal with dishonor and rebellion whenever it presents itself. Christian parents are required by Scripture to use discipline when necessary for, "A child left to himself brings shame to his mother" (Prov. 29:15).

IS IT FAIR?

The question in most people's minds is this: Is it fair to expect little ones to be obedient in these areas? My answer is, "Yes, it is." It does not happen with the snap of a finger. You will have to work at it, just like anything else that matters. They can do it, but they need a good and patient shepherd, who knows where he is going and is not willing to leave any behind.

Unfortunately, in our culture, we have accepted a standard of behavior that allows outright rebellion in toddlers. Don't join that club! The common feeling is that rebellion is normal and acceptable during two periods of life: early childhood and the teen years. So they tell you, "Just close your eyes and it will go away eventually." Mark Twain represented this philosophy very well:

> *"When a child turns 12 you should put him in a barrel, nail a lid down and feed him through a knot hole. When he turns 16 you should seal up the knot hole."*

Not so fast. We need to think outside our own cultural standards about rebellion. Is there any indication from the Bible that rebellion just needs to be tolerated until it goes away? Is rebellion acceptable? Should it be socially acceptable in your home?

PERFECTION NOT NECESSARY

I'm certainly not suggesting that your children need to be perfect. That won't happen. I had plenty of "moments" with my children in church. The question is, what kind of culture are we cultivating? A culture of rebellion?

People in our culture think, "You cannot expect a two-year-old to obey." Unfortunately, this principle is usually a prophesy. You pretty much get what you expect. Those who believe it *is* impossible for young children to be obedient in church, for them, it *will* be impossible.

Here is a dose of reality: when a child can sit still, he is teachable, under authority, and able to exercise self-control. This is a pathway to success in later years. But more importantly, it is the pathway to beholding the "beauty of the Lord."

SELF-CONTROL

Most little children, at some point, will cry so loudly that they need to be taken out of the worship service. Don't be afraid to leave the service to get your children back on track. You should not take them out for every little peep. But if it becomes too distracting for the other worshipers, or if they are flat out rebelling, please do the whole church a favor and take them out.

You need to make it crystal clear that they are not allowed to let their emotions get out of control. This is something you must teach them by telling them, "You are not allowed to act this way, no crying. You may never scream in church (or at home)." It should not be normal to hear the same squalling children every week in church. They must be obedient. Children need to keep self-control and you ought to embrace the principle that it is possible for them to keep it.

Taking your child out of the service will likely be a normal part of child training when they are very young. Don't be embarrassed. Although, if it is happening all the time, you need to take a hard look at how you are handling things at home. Your church experience will normally mirror your home experience.

NOT A PLAY TIME

If you remove your child from the service for discipline, don't make it a play time. Don't make it more fun than the service. It is self-defeating because children know how to work the system. They are not dumb. They might even be naughty so that they are removed to have a play time. This is how children wrap you around their little fingers.

If you take your child out of the service for a few minutes, don't make it a different kind of time than what you have in the main service. One way to do this is to go to another room and have them sit in your lap… and not play. When the child settles down, take them back to the service. Don't be afraid to do this multiple times.

DON'T BRIBE

While I fully acknowledge that God does reward us for obedience, I am cautious about rewarding a child with food, toys, or other incentives for good behavior. I believe this is going in the wrong direction and will eventually take you where you don't want to go. Good behavior should be the baseline. If you start paying them to be polite, you will get a selfish, materialistic brat. And, you might end up paying your children to go to church.

FATHERS PLAY A KEY ROLE

One of the mistakes that fathers can make is delegating all of this work to their wives or older children. My experience is that a common denominator of unrestrainable children in the worship service is often a father who is not taking personal responsibility. Of course, husbands and wives need to work together on this.

We all understand the struggles that arise from keeping your children in church. In the midst of the difficulties, be very patient with one another. You are making disciples of Jesus Christ. You are showing them true treasure. You are telling them of the praises of the Lord, teaching them the ways of gladness, opening the gates of righteousness, and paving the way for everlasting joy. And don't forget that the Holy Spirit is always working beyond your abilities. God and God alone can save your children, giving them hearts to love Him.

This can be messy work. We will need to persevere through successes, failures, and re-takes. And what is at stake? Nothing less than the eternal souls of our children. (Col. 3:20; Eph. 6:1-4).

DISCUSSION

- Which ideas do you need to incorporate for keeping your children with you in church?
- As husband and wife, are you in agreement over the things you need to incorporate?

DISTRACTED CHILDREN

"My heart is steadfast, O God, my heart is steadfast: I will sing and give praise. Awake, my glory; awake, lute and harp: I will awaken the dawn. I will praise You, O Lord, among the people" (Ps. 57:7-9).

Now that you prepared your children for the importance of the moment, and now that they are coming into the church ready to hear, what do you do *during* the service? The answer is this: help them keep their hearts *fixed* on God. Help them be *awake* and stay *awake,* to all the things that worship brings. Remember, you are tour guides for everlasting joy in our Lord Jesus Christ.

DEAL WITH DISTRACTIONS

First of all, let me acknowledge that everyone gets distracted at church. I get distracted. You get distracted. So, don't be too hard on your children when they get distracted. At the same time, you should be attentive to notice when your children are getting distracted and help them get back on track.

David Clarkson says that the "wanderings, rovings of the mind, will, affections, senses, caused by the cares of the world and the lusts of the flesh" are the chief reasons for distractions.[1] He says it is hard to hit the moving object of a distracted soul. One way you can do this with little ones is to

1   Smith, T. (Ed.) (1864). *The Works of David Clarkson, B.D. Vol. 1* (p. 437). Edinburgh, Scotland: James Nichol.

encourage them to listen for particular words and mark down how many times they heard it.

THE WORSHIP SERVICE IS NOT A PLAY TIME—NO TOYS

Playing in church does not teach your children to understand the gravity of worship and the wisdom of being still. I am not in favor of giving children things to play with in church. No rattles or cars, etc. I also discourage reading books other than the Bible. I maintain that allowing children to read other books desensitizes and distracts them from the gravity of the gathering of God's people for worship. If you bring crayons in, then draw outlines of pictures that will help your children participate in the service not get disconnected. Playing in church gives them the impression that the singing, preaching, and praying are not important. You don't want to create a tune-out pattern in your children.

NO WALKING AROUND DURING THE CHURCH SERVICE

Some people think it's ok to allow their children to walk around during church services. Don't do it. It is simply distracting and dishonorable behavior. You would never allow this at a theater, basketball game, or the office of your boss at work. You owe it to the people around you, the pastor, and to the gravity of the moment.

RELAX WITH THEIR DIFFERENT COGNITIVE CAPABILITIES

You will need to be extra attentive to the capacities of each child. Some children can only understand one word or one concept from the sermon. Not a problem! Help your child to understand at least one element of the sermon. Pick one thing from that sermon and discuss it. A child who understands one word or one concept has experienced at least one victory.

Relax. Knowledge is cumulative. Learning is always a slow pile-up of truth. They don't need to hear everything or understand everything. Their understanding of everything was never my goal as a father. My goal was that they would understand at least one thing. Notice the wisdom of Richard Baxter's father:

> "At first my father set me to read the historical parts of the scripture, which suiting with my nature, greatly delighted me; and though all that time I neither understood or relished much the doctrinal part, and mystery of redemption, yet it did me good by acquainting me with the matters of fact, and drawing me on to love the Bible, and to search by degrees into the rest."[2]

BABY STEPS

Parents somehow feel that children need to understand everything that is said. Not so. Baby steps are normal. They don't need to understand everything. Nobody gets everything out of anything. Nobody remembers everything they hear in a sermon. Your children just need to learn a little more than what they knew before—even if it is one new word they did not know before, one new story, or one new illustration in the Word of God. This is what we love about baby steps. The first step sends the whole family to their feet in a standing ovation. Baby steps in sermon acquisition ought to be the same.

---

2   Baxter, R. (1799). *The Life of the Reverend Richard Baxter* (p. 4). London, England: London Religious Tract Society

WORDS

When I had young children, I would have them listen for specific words in the sermon and bump my arm when they heard them. When they learned to write, I would write a word on my notes, and circle it and have them copy it on their own paper for later discussion. At other times, I would have them illustrate the scenes of the sermon text by drawing pictures of it, as the preacher preached his sermon. The Bible is full of illustrations and imagery from nature and real-life experiences. Many sections in your Bible can be illustrated on paper. This is one way to encourage small children to be engaged.

I wanted my children to love the preaching by tracking with the preacher. I wanted them to see that no matter who is preaching, they can strike gold—if they listen carefully. I did not want my children to get the cancer of, "I didn't get anything out of that." Don't let them think that way. Yes, you can get something out of everything! Teach them to have a heart to squeeze every ounce of good out of every sermon.

AWAKEN RESPECT FOR THE PREACHER

Teach your children to engage with the preacher—eyeball to eyeball. One way you can assist them is by developing a culture of respect for the preacher or anyone else who is speaking or leading. Train them to keep their eyes on the preacher. Take notice when they let their eyes wander. Create a culture in your family where its wrong, impolite and unacceptable to talk to each other or look around while the preacher is preaching.

Remember, God designed these moments specifically for their joy. We must never forget that distractions in meetings designed for joy, only dilute gladness. So, do what you can to minimize the distractions and teach your children to mine maximum joy from the means of grace. You are setting them up. You are helping them to say in the genuineness of their hearts, "My heart is fixed O God, my heart is fixed: I will sing and give praise." How did that happen? It happened because somebody came alongside to help shape their conscience by saying, "Awake" (Ps. 57:7).

DISCUSSION

- Do you agree that it is appropriate to help your children to pay attention *during* the service? Do you think it is too disruptive to the meeting to have distracted children?
- What are the ways you can appropriately help your children pay attention at church? What kinds of things have you tried in the past? How do you think they worked?

FELLOWSHIP OF GLADNESS AND SINCERITY OF HEART

"And they continued steadfastly in the apostles' doctrine and fellowship, in the breaking of bread, and in prayers... So continuing daily with one accord in the temple, and breaking bread from house to house, they ate their food with gladness and simplicity of heart, praising God and having favor with all the people" (Acts 2:42, 46-47).

True churches experience authentic community. The biblical word for this is "fellowship." Make sure you show your children the contours of true Christian fellowship that are described in Acts 2:42-47. Open their eyes to a community of love, a fellowship of joy, and the family of the King of kings. Pray and work for them so that they will say:

"But I am like a green olive tree in the house of God; I trust in the mercy of God forever and ever. I will praise You forever, because You have done it; and in the presence of Your saints I will wait on Your name, for it is good" (Ps. 52:8-9).

DEALING WITH UNCONVERTED CHILDREN

If your children are unconverted, they will not be able to experience this kind of Christian fellowship to its fullness. But they will have the opportunity to behold the beauty of a happy, truthful, and merciful community.

When the community is not so happy, truthful, or merciful, your children will see how you responded in love to the difficulties. You can explain from the Scriptures what went wrong. It will be a golden opportunity to show them the glory of God compared to an inglorious man. In this sense, problems in a church should not be a problem. They are simply illustrations of the truth of Scripture—we are fallen creatures who "see through a glass darkly." But, even more than that, these heartbreaking situations are marvelous opportunities to help you shine the light of the Word of God. Perhaps, over time, the Lord will use it to soften their hearts.

THE ORIGIN AND PROGRESS OF THE CHURCH

The whole of Acts 2 shows how the early church was created, and what it looks like on the ground. First, the fellowship of the church was born out of the work of the Holy Spirit on the day of Pentecost. Therefore, it is a spiritual and supernatural community. This means that the kind of fellowship in the church is much deeper than the fellowship you have with the folks at the gym. The "fellowship" that true Christians experience is spiritual, and the four activities mentioned in Acts 2:42 are enlivened by the Holy Spirit.

There are four things the Holy Spirit caused the church to engage in. First, the apostles' teaching. Second, fellowship. Third, the breaking of bread. Fourth, prayer. It is the Holy Spirit that fills all these activities. They come alive by supernatural power. The Holy Spirit supercharges them. He makes them a joy. Of course, these things can be performed lifelessly or heartlessly by rote. Anybody can duplicate dead legalistic teaching, fellowship, breaking of bread and prayer. Anybody can be dull. Rather, it is the Holy Spirit that makes these things come alive with spiritual power.

Notice *how* the Holy Spirit gives these things a depth of quality and pathos. First, it flows out of "gladness and sincerity of heart," and second, it is performed "steadfastly." They were "praising God." In other words, their fellowship was full of joy and it was done passionately and regularly. It was a big part of their lives. They loved it because the Holy Spirit is the spirit of "love, joy, peace, patience, kindness, goodness, faithfulness, gentleness, and self-control" (Gal. 5:22-23).

TRIALS

Yes, there are trials in local churches. Disagreements and offenses will arise in every local church. But God has shown us how to work our way through them by looking to the truth of the Word of God and obeying it. In other words, the bonds we have are bigger than simply liking one another, appreciating one another, and feeling "connected." They are spiritual bonds. All of the conflicts are meant to increase your love, compassion, wisdom, patience, and joy—all of which is done by applying the truth of the Word of God in the power of the Holy Spirit.

A LITTLE FORETASTE

J.C. Ryle captures at least one element of these benefits as he writes about the special nature of the church and the joys which exist there:

> *"Who, indeed, can describe the pleasure with which the members of Christ's flock do meet each other face to face? They may have been strangers before. They may have lived apart and never been in company; but it is wonderful to observe how soon they seem to understand each other. There seems a thorough oneness of opinion, taste, and judgment so that a man would think they had known each other for years.*

> *They seem, indeed, to feel they are servants of one and the same Master, members of the same family, and have been converted by one and the same Spirit. They have one Lord, one faith, one baptism. They have the same trials, the same fears, the same doubts, the same temptations, the same faintings of heart, the same dread of sin, the same sense of unworthiness, the same love of their Savior. Oh, but there is a mystical union between true believers, which they only know who have experienced it. The world cannot understand it—it is all foolishness to them. But that union does really exist, and a most blessed thing it is; for it is like a little foretaste of heaven.*
>
> *Beloved, this loving to be together is a special mark of Christ's flock—nor is it strange, if we consider they are walking in the same narrow way and fighting against the same deadly enemies—and never are they so happy as when they are in company. The unconverted know nothing of such happiness."[1]*

I pray you will experience what Ryle describes. I hope your local church will be for you a little "foretaste of heaven," and a happiness, "with gladness and simplicity of heart, praising God and having favor with all the people."

DISCUSSION

- In what ways have you managed to help your children taste and see that the Lord is good in the fellowship of the saints?
- Make a list of the things you need to do to ratchet up your children's joy for the fellowship of the saints in the teaching, fellowship, breaking of bread, and prayer.

---

1 Ryle, J.C. (2002) *The Christian Race and Other Sermons* (pp. 94-95) Moscow, ID: Charles Nolan Publishers.

JOYFUL SINGING

"Let the word of Christ dwell in you richly in all wisdom, teaching and admonishing one another in psalms and hymns and spiritual songs, singing with grace in your hearts to the Lord" (Col. 3:16).

The Bible makes it clear that God wants to draw your family to sing of the greatness of God and the salvation that is in Jesus Christ. It may surprise you to hear this, but Christian parents are divinely appointed singing teachers. It is another one of your duties that is designed to spread joy in your home. The Bible commands it, "shout for joy," sing in the morning, and sing under the "shadow of [His] wings" (Ps. 5:11; Ps. 59:16; Ps. 63:7). An entire Psalm is dedicated to singing on the Lord's Day. In Psalm 92:

"It is good to give thanks to the Lord, and to sing praises to Your name, O Most High; to declare your lovingkindness in the morning, and Your faithfulness every night...to declare that the Lord is upright; He is my rock, and there is no unrighteousness in Him."

You are appointed by God to be the jurisdictional movers and shakers on the Lord's Day (Ex. 20:8-11). You are responsible for making it happen according to God's design. Singing is part of that design. This is rolled up in your responsibility to instruct your children, by bringing "them up in the training and admonition of the Lord."

THE BIBLE TELLS ME SO

You need to teach your children to sing because the Bible teaches you to sing. We sing not only because we discovered a blessing, but because a wise and faithful God has instructed us to do it.

In addition, singing connects children's hearts with God, His truth, and His joy. This means that you have a wonderful opportunity to increase the joy of your children. In doing so, you are helping them to avoid a meaningless life. Singing is one way that we protect our children from living thoughtlessly, lifelessly, and joylessly.

Singing can be worth more than counseling sessions, more than money, more than friends, and more than books. Singing can be the best antidote to pride, hurt feelings, and sin.

In Nehemiah 12, we see that a month after the wall of Jerusalem was finished, the Jews were looking back in joyful celebration of what God had done over the last 100 years. Having identified with the reformation which God had wrought among them, all the people—women and children included—rose up to dedicate themselves in joyful obedience. "Also that day they offered great sacrifices, and rejoiced, for God had made them rejoice with great joy; the women and the children also rejoiced, so that the joy of Jerusalem was heard afar off" (Neh. 12:43).

In his book *The Religious Affections*, Jonathan Edwards explained the importance of singing:

> *"And the **duty of singing** praises to God, seems to be appointed wholly to excite and express religious affections. No other reason can be assigned, why we should express ourselves to God in verse, rather than in prose, and do it with music, but only, that such is our nature and frame, that these things have a tendency to move our affections."*[1]

---

1   Edwards, J. (2001). *The Religious Affections* (p. 44). Edinburgh, Scotland: Banner of Truth.

Martin Luther gave testimony to this as well:

> *"Music is a fair and lovely gift of God which has often wakened and moved me to the joy of preaching . . . Music drives away the devil and makes people gay (happy) . . . Next after theology I give to music the highest place and the greatest honor."*[2]

REMEMBER WHAT SINGING CAN DO

A hardened heart can be softened as God applies the biblical truth contained in the Psalms, hymns and spiritual songs. Singing softens the soil of the heart and prepares children to receive the gospel. Once they are born again, singing helps them to rejoice in the goodness of God. Singing is a medicine from heaven. Preaching excites the mind but singing revives the heart.

Singing is for children. Isaac Watts acknowledged this in his hymn *Jesus Shall Reign*:

> *People and realms from every tongue*
> *Dwell on His love with sweetest song*
> *And infant voices shall proclaim*
> *Their early blessings of His name.*[3]

You want your children to be singing of "their early blessings of His name," for decades to come.

HOW TO RESPOND IF THEY RESIST SINGING

It is very important that your children participate fully in singing. But what if your children don't like to sing, avoid

---

2   Bainton, R.H. (2013). *Here I Stand: A Life of Martin Luther* (p. 352). Nashville, TN: Abingdon Press.

3   Sims, W.H. (Ed.) (1956). *Baptist Hymnal* (no. 116). Nashville, TN: Convention Press

singing, or simply refuse to sing? If this is your situation, I would like to encourage you to do two things:

First, your initial impulse should be to help them to love it. Inspire them. Come alongside. Be a compassionate and patient high priest who has his goals in mind and who stays on plan. Don't give up! If you love it, they will find it easier to love it. Make it fun. Sing in the car, at dinner time and bedtime... Make it beautiful and sing beautiful music. Help them taste the joy.

Second, don't let them off the hook. They need to know that God commands them to sing. He gave clear instructions. It is legitimate for parents to say, happily and graciously, compassionately and gently yet firmly, "We sing because God commanded us to sing and He loves to hear it." The Lord teaches us that the church is supposed to sing and you should teach your family in like manner.

The apostle Paul taught at least two young churches, not only to sing but also, how to sing. He teaches us that the church sings.

It is easy to allow children to be uninvolved, disengaged, listless, and pointless singers. Parents need to come to the rescue. I bet your children can sing the latest theme song from their favorite movie—with gusto. Don't let your children sing any way they want. Teach them to rise up and sing with all their hearts.

Children need to know that they are not allowed to make up their own version of life. You help them make a life. Build a culture. Lay down godly patterns. Teach them to sing. But how? The next chapter will explain.

DISCUSSION

- What are the joys of singing?
- What barriers stand in the way of your family becoming a singing family?

TEACHING CHILDREN ᵀᴼ SING

"Blessed are the people who know the joyful sound! They walk, O Lord, in the light of Your countenance" (Ps. 89:15).

Make sure you use the Bible to teach your children how to sing in church. Singing is powerful because it teaches us doctrine and is a means of self-conscious unity. It puts us in a disposition of praise and casts us into a sea of hope. Singing helps us deal with our fears, hurts, and cares, and teaches us to be a thankful people.

A SINGING FAMILY

The church is a big family that sings. Singing is like a team sport. Like all team sports, the team members need to know their parts. It is something that we do *with* others and *for* others in the church. It is not something we do primarily for ourselves—even though it is wonderfully helpful to our hearts. It is very important that when we "enter into His gates with thanksgiving" (Ps. 100:4) that we know what we are doing and why we are doing it.

WHAT SPECIFIC THINGS DO YOU NEED TO TEACH YOUR FAMILY?

They Need to Know What They Are Doing When They Sing

Here are seven things to teach your children about what we are doing when we sing:

1. They are declaring what we believe.
2. They are singing their doctrine.
3. They are describing the nature of the God they worship.
4. They are affirming the kind of gospel they are proclaiming.
5. They are acknowledging what God wants from them and wants to do in them.
6. They are announcing what is their greatest comfort in life and death.
7. Singing unites them in the truth that changes their lives.

We love to do these things because they proclaim the commonality of our experience in what has happened to us.

They Need to Know What God Is Doing

God is desiring to move your children. He wants to grip their hearts. Singing is beautifully designed to communicate the beauty of the Lord. Here are five ways God wants to direct your minds and grip your hearts as you sing. Teach these things to your children so that they do what God commands. You want them to grow up singing with the richness that God has designed.

First, Teach Them to Sing to Teach Others God's Truth

The church must be a teaching church. Our teaching does not only come through preaching, it also comes through our singing (Col. 3:16; Eph. 5:19; John 4:24).

You ought to show your children that they are teaching others while they are singing. When we sing, God teaches us through one another, "Let the word of Christ dwell in you richly in all wisdom, teaching and admonishing one another in psalms and hymns and spiritual songs, singing with grace in your hearts to the Lord" (Col. 3:16). When we sing, we teach one another from the "Word of Christ." This is referring to singing biblical truth. As we sing, we are teaching sound doctrine. The words "dwell richly" indicate a depth of saturation by the Word of Christ, letting it take root, drinking in the richness of truth.

This is in sharp contrast to some of the manifestations of Christian worship services where you get lost in your own personal emotions. Yes, emotions are involved in Christian singing, but if the mind is turned off, it is not Christian worship.

In pagan worship, you lose yourself in a self-centered altered state of repetition. It easily devolves to nothing more than self-centered emotional ecstasy. Unfortunately, many people judge a worship service on how emotional they were when they were singing, not by the truth they were singing. The Holy Spirit is the Spirit of truth, and when the Spirit is speaking, He is always speaking the truth.

Pagan worship makes an idol of emotions. Lifeless conservative worship can make an idol of doctrine to the absence of emotions. God has designed us to need both doctrine and emotion. This is why He commands both. God calls for the whole man to participate. True Christian worship is both thoughtful and emotional.

Second, Teach Them to Sing to Admonish One Another

Paul says that we sing, "admonishing one another." He uses the Greek word *noutheteo*. In English, this means to warn and instruct. It is often a means of correcting one another. In this sense, singing is an action that seeks to move someone from one position to another. It is a warning and re-directing. Our hearts need re-direction (Col. 3:16). This is one way that we "sing with understanding" (1 Cor. 14:15). Our minds are activated by singing.

Third, Teach Them to Sing to God Personally

Paul directs the Colossian church to sing "psalms and hymns and spiritual songs… to the Lord" (Col. 3:16). Paul told the Ephesian church to be "making melody in your heart to the Lord, giving thanks always for all things to God the Father in the name of our Lord Jesus Christ" (Eph. 5:19-20). Therefore, one aspect of singing is that we sing directly and personally "to the Lord." It is very much like prayer. Teach your children to sing directly and prayerfully to the Lord when the song is written that way. Augustine said, "He who sings prays twice." Singing is a cleansing agent for filling our minds and healing our emotions (Col. 3:16).

Fourth, Teach Them to Sing to the Unconverted Among You

When we sing, we are confessing the name of Christ to those who are unbelievers among us. Paul says, "I will confess you among the Gentiles and sing unto your name" (Rom. 15:9). He also speaks to the Corinthian church about how harmful it is to speak things that cannot be understood by the unbelievers in the meeting: "there come in those who are uninformed or unbelievers, will they not say that you are out of your mind?" Rather, they should be able to understand what is being spoken through a "Psalm or a teaching." Then the "unbeliever" or "uninformed person" hears it and is "convinced" and "convicted by all." As a result, he worships God, "And then he will go away saying, God is truly among you" (1 Cor. 14:23-25).

When the unbeliever comes into the church, he is observing everything. He takes it all in. He looks around. He makes judgments. He learns what makes these church people tick. The singing shows him what they love, what they think, and how they feel. Their singing is a display of Christian life, of doctrine, of emotions, and of love. When you sing, you are declaring to them what makes you tick in your thinking and in your feeling.

When we are at church, we should lift up our voices and sing also to the Gentiles. We shouldn't let one note be lost for the sake of the lost among us. Let them see and hear that His praise is glorious. Let them see that He makes you happy. Let them see that He carries you through your sorrows. Make it clear that, "He has made me glad" (Ps. 122:1). Shout out that He is a healing salve for every soul. Let it flow out of your heart. Let it come because you love lost people. It's such a beautiful thing to sing with all your heart.

Fifth, Teach Them to Sing to Their Own Souls

In the Psalms, David is singing to his soul:

> *"Bless the Lord, O my soul; and all that is within me, bless His holy name! Bless the Lord, O my soul, and forget not all His benefits: who forgives all your iniquities, who heals all your diseases, who redeems your life from destruction, who crowns you with lovingkindness and tender mercies…" (Ps. 103:1-4).*

Sometimes we need to sing to our own souls. David is referring to the inner man. We need to sing to our inward thoughts and attitudes. We need to tell our inner being to "Bless the Lord" instead of meditating on our troubles. We need a soul adjustment (Ps. 103:1-4). Martin Luther said, "Music drives away the devil and makes people happy" (*Here I Stand*, 266). Make your instruction on this matter so clear that they will never forget that through singing Jesus wants their souls to be happy.

TWO FINAL ADMONITIONS

First, let me review the basics above. Teach your children that they have a responsibility to sing. If they are mumbling the songs or not singing at all, then you ought to teach them that they must sing. They don't get to do their own thing in the church. Don't let them be selfishly silent. God has commanded them to lift up their voices for the benefit of the whole church. After all, we are not allowed to let our children be selfish.

Second, teach your children to sing in the voice the song is written. Is the song sung in the voice of teaching or admonition? Is it sung personally to God, or is it a personal and corporate testimony about God? Is it a song that you sing to your own soul, or a declaration of truth to the unbeliever? Help them sing it that way. Guide them to sing intentionally, thoughtfully, relationally, and evangelistically—in the voice the song is written.

Remember that the Bible teaches that singing in a Christian manner is to sing with a depth of understanding and feeling. It is self-conscious and intentional. It is relationally connected and emotionally rich. It moves the heart. It is intellectually deep, theologically sound, and evangelistically self-conscious. It is explicitly pedagogical. The majesty of God is revealed. The joy of the Lord is the result. It can be literally, soul transforming.

TEACH THE WAY OF HAPPINESS

So teach your children to sing. Teach them to sing well. Help them to think deeply about what they are singing. Singing helps us to be a thoughtful and happy people. It is a gift to make the heart happy.

Think of the times when you catch yourself humming a song. Why are you doing that? Well, you probably heard someone in your home singing or humming it, you unconsciously caught it, and now you are singing it. Joy spreads this way in a family. When this happens, I hope what you hear are the songs of the joys of the kingdom of God and the work of His Son.

And who knows, God might save your children as they sing of Christ and His beauty. And, sometime in the future, if they are born again, those songs will ring in their ears like never before. They will find that they have become the happy ones "who know the joyful sound."

DISCUSSION

- Are your children singing when the church sings, or are they disengaged?
- Is there anything you need to do to increase the involvement, understanding, and vigor in singing among your children?

LISTENING ᴛᴏ SERMONS

"So then faith comes by hearing, and hearing by the Word of God" (Rom. 10:17).

A s we engage the critical matter of listening to sermons, we must first acknowledge that h*ow* your child hears will determine *where* he will spend eternity.

Because faith comes by hearing the Word of God, I hope you and your children spend hundreds of hours in church listening to sermons. Not kiddie sermons or "sermonettes for Christianettes." Be a good tour guide through the sermons they hear. Do everything you can to make it a rich experience. Make it your aim to increase the joy in their hearts. May they feel like Jeremiah who said, "Your word to me was the joy and the rejoicing of my heart" (Jer. 15:16), and David who exclaimed, "Your testimonies are my delight" (Ps. 119:24), "How sweet are your words to my taste" (Ps. 119:103), "Your statutes have been my songs" (Ps 119:54), "more to be desired than gold," and "sweeter also than honey and the honeycomb" (Ps. 19:10).

Do what you can to help them hear the Word of God throughout the whole sermon. Jesus says, "Take heed how you hear" (Luke 8:18). Children need to learn how to "Take heed." Taking heed is an action you take. It means to pay attention, be ready, and take notice. This means that your children need *your* help to teach them how to hear. You are teaching them to do something. They need coaching and assistance. Train them to listen. This is your job as a parent.

Here is my appeal: have a strategy for what you will do before, during, and after the sermon each Sunday to help you and your children listen. You are teaching them a life skill.

Passivity is not your friend nor your children's friend. It's not a friend of hearing. Rise up. Help them love the Lord through the sermons.

Here are six ways for making the most of the preaching experience, beginning at home. It takes some preparation and time getting your hearts ready.

FIRST, EXAMINE YOUR OWN HEART— IS IT A JOY FOR YOU?

Your joyful delight in the Word of God is infectious. And don't forget—your listless, dispassionate listening is even more infectious. Follow the example of David and lead your whole family to say, "I was glad when they said unto me let us go into the house of the Lord" (Ps. 122:1). Do you, "Enter into His gates with thanksgiving and His courts with praise" (Ps. 100:4)? Do you say what Nehemiah said, "We will not neglect the house of God" (Neh. 10:39)? In our home, we would often set the tone for our Sunday morning by preparing on Saturday night. We wanted to make sure we did not fill the evening with movies, entertainments, and get-togethers. We realized that the more high-octane entertainment we fed our children, the less they would appreciate preaching. On Sunday morning, we would have worshipful music playing as we bustled around the house getting ready for church. It helped all of us to prepare our hearts.

SECOND, GET FOCUSED ON MIND EXPANSION

Sermons are mind-expanding and soul-satisfying for believing children. They are also mind-expanding for unbelieving children, and they prepare the way for faith.

When you require unbelieving children to listen to sermons, you are giving them reasons to believe. This is why sermons are necessary for child development. I want to convince you that sermons should be an important focus of the discipleship and preparation of children to receive the gospel. Sermons stimulate minds, improve vocabulary, introduce complex concepts, and foment intellectual activity. Parents need to capture the opportunity with vigor. The Word of God is "sharper than any two-edged sword" (Heb. 4:12).

The regular preaching of the Word of God is a powerful tool for transformation in a family. It shapes the culture of your home. This is only one reason why you must gather all the generations together for the preaching of the Word of God.

THIRD, FAMILIARIZE YOUR FAMILY WITH THE SERMON TEXT BEFORE THE PREACHING

Do what is necessary to find out what Scripture text the pastor is going to be preaching from. To accomplish this in our local church, we have a weekly men's Bible study for this express purpose. We want our men to teach their families what the upcoming Scripture text is all about before the pastor preaches on it. We meet early in the morning at the beginning of the week and discuss the text. We do this to help our men understand what the text is saying. We desire that everyone in the church will come to worship on Sunday already having reviewed the terminology, theology, and the central message of the passage. We want them to work through it beforehand and to arrive at some practical applications for their families. If you don't have a men's Bible study like this, you can simply ask your pastor what he is preaching on and then help your family understand it before they hear it. Your pastor will be delighted to know you are doing this.

FOURTH, PREPARE YOUR FAMILY TO HEAR

In Luke 19:48, we find a people "very attentive to hear Him." It is extremely important that you help your children to be attentive—very attentive. Help them learn how to hear sermons. Why? Hearing the Word of God is a matter of life and death.

This is why you ought to intentionally prepare your family to hear the sermon. Much has been written on "How to listen to a sermon." Let me paraphrase George Whitefield's instructions for hearing sermons: Come with a sincere desire to know your duty. Pray before, during, and after the sermon. Listen to the sermon as if you are listening to a king, as the Lord of lords Himself. Why? Because ministers are sent from God. They are ambassadors who speak the words of God. Do not think poorly of the minister when you think of his weaknesses.[1]

FIFTH, CAST A VISION FOR THE IMPORTANCE OF THE MOMENT

It is critical that you impress on your children the importance of the moment. God has always gathered His people together to worship Him. Coming to God's house is a holy and God-ordained moment. *It is the most important meeting scheduled all week.* Help your children see the priority and importance of the gatherings of God's people to hear preaching. Help them

---

1   Whitefield, G. (n.d.). *How to Listen to a Sermon*. Retrieved August 29, 2020, from https://www.monergism.com/thethreshold/articles/onsite/howtolisten.html

sense the prioritization, the expectation, and the privilege of the moment. If you sense they are like those who, "shrugged their shoulders and stiffened their necks and would not hear" (Neh. 9:29), then wake up! Snap into action. Help them learn to appreciate it out of your own infectious zeal and your intrusive involvement.

SIXTH, PRAY FOR THE PREACHER BEFORE THE CHURCH SERVICE

Take time to give thanks for the preacher and the preparation he has engaged in. Preaching is labor. Most of the time, it is *hard* labor—and often torturous. After studying their sermon text during the week, most pastors languish and cry out to God into the late hours of the night and the early hours of the morning before they preach. They feel profoundly inadequate. They desire with all their hearts to accurately and effectually represent God and His Word. They want to be a blessing to their hearers, but they know they will fall short in every way. They need your prayers.

To connect the hearts of your children to your pastor, get to know him in a personal way. Have him to your home for dinner. This will make him more real to your children.

PRACTICAL HELP

Help your children succeed in church. Here are some practical ideas:

- Speak to them about what's ahead on Sunday before they fall asleep in bed on Saturday evening.
- Make sure they get a good sleep.
- Feed them healthy food in the morning avoiding sugar and caffeine.

- Make sure they use the restroom just before you depart for the church.

Teach your children to love the preaching. Help them to listen. Perhaps someday they will be like those who "welcomed it not as the word of men, but as it is in truth, the word of God" (1 Thess. 2:13).

Cry out to God that they will have Jeremiah's experience:

"Your words were found, and I ate them, and Your word was to me the joy and rejoicing of my heart; for I am called by Your name, O LORD God of hosts" (Jer. 15:16).

Faith comes by hearing the word of God.

DISCUSSION

- How would you rate the attentiveness of your child to the preaching?
- What specifically can you do to help your children listen before the service, during the service, and after the service?

APPLYING SERMONS

"The words of the wise are like goads, and the words of scholars are like well-driven nails, given by one Shepherd" (Ecc. 12:11).

Sermons are like "goads." They were designed to inform as well as move you forward. Goads stimulate movement. In Israel, they were sharp pointed objects that were used to move cattle from one place to another. Matthew Poole describes these goads as, "piercing into men's dull minds and hard hearts, and quickening and provoking them to practice of all their duties."[1] In this sense, the Word of God is meant to move people forward. One way pastors do this is to stimulate their people to make the most of what's happening—including the good, the bad, and the ugly. This is why you should discuss the sermon with your family afterward. Milk it for all it is worth. Yes, I've said this already and may say it again. Get out the miner's tools and keep digging. Squeeze every ounce of good out of it. Let the words be like goads that move them to action. Drive the nails home with practical application.

Satan is always at the door to steal the sown Word of God (Mark 4:15). The devil is always on standby. You may be passive, but the devil is never passive. In his hand are fiery darts to incinerate the words of God. He would make you and your children deaf, dumb, and blind to the Word of God. Do all you can to hinder him. He is a lying and deceiving snake.

---

1   Poole, M. (1968). *A Commentary on the Holy Bible, Vol. 2* (p. 307). London, England: Banner of Truth.

David Clarkson, commenting on the parable of the hearers (soils), says that:

> *"There are many enemies to oppose, and many impediments to hinder you in hearing...from ourselves, Satan, the world, afflictions, allurements; blindness, ignorance in the mind..."*[2]

He points out that "Hearing is the provision made for the soul's eternal well-being, its everlasting welfare depends upon it; if you fail here, your souls perish without remedy."[3]

DISCUSS

Make it your practice to talk about the sermons *the day you hear them.* Don't let them fly away into the air by neglect. Seize the moment. Delay is a tool of the devil. As *you* delay, *he* is not delaying. He is stealing, killing, and destroying. God Himself had a purpose in what you heard in the preaching. Take it seriously. Make a big deal about it. Review it when you get home from church. Prioritize it like you do food:

> *"I have treasured the words of His mouth more than my necessary food" (Job 23:12).*

Our regular practice in the Brown family is to discuss the sermon at dinnertime on Sunday. We go around the table and each person shares something that struck them. As Richard Baxter says, "Chew the cud, and call up all when you come home in secret."[4]

---

2   Smith, T. (Ed.) (1864). *The Works of David Clarkson, B.D. Vol. 1* (p. 429). Edinburgh, Scotland: James Nichol

3   Smith, T. (Ed.) (1864). *The Works of David Clarkson, B.D. Vol. 1* (p. 431). Edinburgh, Scotland: James Nichol

4   Baxter, R. (1990). *The Practical Works of Richard Baxter, Vol. 1:*

Patrick Henry, the great statesman of the American War for Independence, delivered the famous speech saying, "Give me liberty or give me death." He attended the sermons of the Great Awakening preacher Samuel Davies. When he was a boy, his mother required him to recount the sermon on the walk home from church every Sunday. She even made him replicate the intensities, inflections, and flourishes of the preacher that morning.

Consider making it your pattern to use the afternoon or evening meal together to discuss the sermon. You might simply ask, "What wondrous things did you hear this morning in the sermon?" Require everyone to have something to share, but they cannot copy the others. They must come with something fresh.

MEMORIZE

Get everyone together and memorize something short from the sermon. It is helpful to pick out a phrase from the Scripture studied during the service. There might be a phrase or concept from the pastor's sermon that would be fun to memorize. Take the time to commit it to memory. Make it short and sweet.

RISE UP

You must rise up and lead your family in order to make your local church a critical discipleship tool.

Making the most of the preaching does not start in the pew. It starts at home and ends at home. Take action. Remove the things that hinder your children from listening in church. Help your children to hear the Word of God. Be diligent.

A Christian Directory. (p. 475). Ligonier, PA: Soli Deo Gloria Publications.

You can be sure of this: Satan *will* be diligent. He is always scheming to steal the Word of God from their hearts. He will capitalize on every distraction and every affection they've nurtured. He delights in your laziness. Parents, resist the devil so that your child is the one "who hears the word and understands it, who indeed bears fruit and produces: some a hundredfold, some sixty, some thirty" (Matt. 13:23). Jesus is speaking of the blessings of truth that takes hold. These are the "well driven nails, given by one Shepherd" (Ecc. 12:11).

DISCUSSION

- List the things you are doing to drive the nails deep and secure.
- What are some of the ways the devil has been robbing you of the biblical truth you are hearing?

PRAYER MEETINGS

"I will make them joyful in my house of prayer"
(Isa. 56:7; Matt. 21:13; Mark 11:17).

P rayer is one of God's gateways to joy for your family. Our Lord Jesus Christ, the most joyful of all the disciples (Heb. 1:9), taught His disciples to pray and so should you teach your children (Matt. 6:9-13). Do it for joy, "…ask, and ye shall receive, that your joy may be full" (John 16:24).

I once heard someone say that a prayerless Christian is like the bus driver trying to push his bus. He does not ask for help, and he does not know that Superman has been on the bus the whole time. We often live helpless lives because we do not pray for help. We do not pray to the only One who can help. Rather, it is such a joy to be able to see and say, "my help comes from the Lord, who made heaven and earth" (Ps. 121:2).

Here is my threefold advice in three action items:

1. Pray as a family at home, as God's fury rests on families that do not pray together (Jer. 10:25).
2. Bring your children to the prayer meetings of the church… but not haphazardly or unprepared. God calls families and churches to pray together. Even the Lord's Prayer pictures corporate prayer, not private prayer.
3. Bring your children with you when you go to pray with others, as they did in Acts 21:5:

> *"When we had come to the end of those days,*
> *we departed and went on our way; and they all*

> *accompanied us, with wives and children, till we were out of the city. And we knelt down on the shore and prayed" (Acts 21:5).*

YOUR RESPONSIBILITY

It is for you as parents to teach your children to pray. This requires that you *prepare them* for real-world prayer sessions. You need to *take them to the prayer meetings.* Our children need us to shepherd them through the experience. When? It begins in the home. Children should first be taught to pray at home.

At home, we teach them the joys of prayer. This includes how not to pray silly prayers, long prayers, unwise prayers, self-serving prayers, or prayers to attract attention to themselves out of pride. Teaching them at home roots out problems so that inappropriate things don't come into the corporate prayer meetings of the church. Oftentimes, having small ones repeat prayers after you can help them learn what is appropriate.

Our church meets for prayer every Wednesday night. There are many children in the prayer meeting. While I am extremely thankful for the large turnout we have, I'm especially thankful that children are there. I want it to be a time of joy for them. I am aware, however, of how uninteresting it can be for them. I especially feel compassion for the parents, for how difficult it can be to make it interesting and also a joy. It is challenging for parents, especially with young children, to navigate corporate prayer meetings.

SIX WAYS PARENTS CAN PREPARE THEIR CHILDREN FOR JOY

1. **Teach Them That This Is What the People of God Are Supposed to Do**

One of the marks of the early church was that they prayed together. Families and children are mentioned in prayer meetings in Acts 1:12-14, 2:42 and 21:4-6. Help your children to see how the family of God is a family that prays together, "My house shall be called a house of prayer" (Matt. 21:13).

When the apostle Peter declared in his sermon, "This promise is for you and your children," and the Lord said, "In you, all the families will be blessed," he was talking about the work of Jesus Christ in His people through salvation. Yet, it also implies the many and various ways God blesses them. One of those ways is through prayer—as a big family.

2. **Keep Them by Your Side in the Prayer Meetings During the Stages of Their Development—Even the Little Years**

My opinion is that God desires that the little ones be present in the prayer meetings of the church. If you have babies-in-arms or toddlers or four-year-olds, recognize that God made them the way they are, and it is okay. Notice what they can learn:

- They will learn that we need God; He is good, and He listens. If this is all they learn by going to the prayer meetings, would you be satisfied? Of course, you would. This would be extremely helpful to them for the rest of their lives.
- They can gain impressions about the spirit of the people. They will hear people pray about their concerns, hurts,

141

desires, victories, and joys. They will be transported from self-obsession into the lives of others.

- They learn how to sit still and respect the desires of their fathers and mothers. This is a critical part of their development because children need practice in the area of honor and obedience. A prayer meeting is a wonderful context in which honor and obedience are cultivated over a long period of time. Prayer meetings offer lots of opportunities for instruction and self-control.

Further, children need to learn how to endure things that are not full-blown entertainment. In our entertainment-saturated culture, we think that everyone must always be riveted and hyped. A prayer meeting provides an opportunity to exist in the midst of God's people without hype. The whole family will be healthier and happier for it. Now, if your children have been shaped by entertainment through visual media, you may have an uphill battle. Their affections are easily controlled by these things, making prayer meetings seem boring. Too much media exposure can be harmful to people who ought to be in prayer meetings. Both children and adults are exposed to way too much hyped entertainment. These things should be severely limited.

3. Prepare Your Children by Showing the Different Ways You Pray When You Gather

The easiest way to explain this is to use the common acronym, ACTS.

- **Adoration**: We pray to adore the Lord and give thanks to Him—we want to be an adoring people.
- **Confession**: We pray in humility, recognizing our sinfulness—we want to be an honest people who confess our sins.

- **Thanksgiving**: We pray to be a thankful people who do not take for granted what God has done and is doing.
- **Supplication**: We pray to come to the aid of others in need.

I will add one more element to ACTS. Add another "S" for Scripture. Pray the words of Scripture. Praying the actual words of God in the Bible is to pray "in Jesus' name" for the things God desires. If your children can read, encourage them to pray the words of Scripture. It is very helpful to teach them the prayers that appear in the Bible. (Here are a few: Matt. 6:9-13; Eph. 3:14-21; Col. 1:9-12; Ps. 51:7-12; Hab. 3:2; Luke 18:13; 1 Chron. 4:10; Ps. 3.)

4. **Prepare Your Children for the Specific Situations to Be Prayed About**

Explain to your children that we are going to pray for different situations that we find ourselves in as a church. We pray for one another—our hurts and joys. We pray for missionaries, people in need, various ministries, local evangelism, and the preaching on Sunday morning, etc. Encourage them to listen for prayers about these things. Give them information beforehand about what's happening in your church. Talk with them about some of the needs in your church. Encourage them to listen for the needs of other people. After the prayer meeting, ask them what categories of prayer they heard.

5. **Help Your Children Be in "One Accord" with the Church**

Inspire them to pursue unity. One way to prepare your children for the prayer meeting is at dinner time just before the prayer meeting. Take some time to help them see that you are one body, gathering for one purpose. Explain that in prayer, all are pulling in the same direction as a big family. This is what they did in the early church, "These all continued with one accord in prayer and supplication, with the women and Mary the mother of Jesus, and with his brothers" (Acts 1:14).

One of the most helpful ways to keep us praying in "one accord" is to say "Amen" after each prayer, either silently or out loud. In our church, we encourage people to say, "Amen" out loud. Saying "Amen" is not the same as saying, "Okay, now we are done praying." To say "Amen" is to agree with the person who prayed. It is the equivalent of saying, "May it be as you have prayed," or "Yes, Lord" (2 Cor. 1:20). Saying "Amen" out loud or in your heart, keeps you focused and unified in the prayer you just heard. It is associated with praise in 1 Chronicles 16:36. Moses instructed the people to say "Amen" at the reading of the blessings and curses that would fall on the people for their obedience or disobedience: "And all the people shall say Amen" (Deut. 27:15-26). In this sense, prayer unifies the church.

6. Help Your Children Fight Distraction

Ask them to notice who is praying and what they are praying about. Teach them to listen carefully and pray along with the person who is praying.

If they are really little, one way to keep them attentive is by whispering in their ear that we are praying for a certain person or situation. This can shake them out of their distraction. This is especially easy if you are holding a little one.

Here is some advice for those of you with lots of little ones:

- Have all of your children pray with you at home, from the oldest to the smallest. The more that they are involved, the more they will enjoy and appreciate it.
- Before an evening prayer meeting, let your children have a later nap than normal.
- Have an easy dinner that is not too heavy.
- Have an older mom and dad in the church help you with the smallest ones while you help your older children learn how to listen and sit still.
- Stay in close proximity to your children. It is best to have adults sitting next to children, so that children sitting next to children do not distract one another. This is a huge challenge for those with lots of little ones.
- Don't let your children make faces at other children in the room—which all children are prone to do.

Like our Lord Jesus taught His disciples, you should teach your children to pray. Help your children engage in corporate prayer in a God-honoring way. In some ways, it is very simple. Teach them how to listen carefully to the prayers.

One of the ways that Satan sabotages the joy of the Lord, is through prayerlessness. This is why Paul instructed the Ephesians to be "rejoicing in hope, patient in tribulation, continuing steadfastly in prayer" (Rom. 12:12). This is how prayer preserves hope in tribulation. He instructed the saints in Philippi, "Rejoice in the Lord always. Again I will say, rejoice!" (Phil. 4:4).

Then Paul made a promise:

"Be anxious for nothing, but in everything by prayer and supplication, with thanksgiving, let your requests be made known to God; and the peace of God, which surpasses all understanding, will guard your hearts and minds through Christ Jesus" (Phil. 4:7).

Teach your children to pray—for their joy.

DISCUSSION

- Have you properly instructed your children on how to pray and how not to pray?
- Have you done anything to lead your children think that church prayer times are an adults-only experience?

THE ORDINANCES <u>OF THE</u> LORD'S SUPPER <u>AND</u> BAPTISM

"The cup of blessing which we bless, is it not the communion of the blood of Christ? The bread which we break, is it not the communion of the body of Christ? For we, though many, are one bread and one body; for we all partake of that one bread" (1 Cor. 10:16-17).

God has given the church two very graphic and beautiful ordinances to help you explain the gospel—The Lord's Supper and Baptism. They both require careful and detailed explanations so that whenever they are performed, your children are connecting them to the joys of salvation. It is a very helpful pedagogy that both ordinances engage the whole body.

These two ordinances draw us into multi-sensory illustrations of the grace of God. They are the perfect ordinances with which to explain the gospel of Jesus Christ to your children. They experientially engage the senses—of hearing, seeing, touching, and tasting. They draw you into the engagement of the entire body.

CONTRASTS

The Lord's Supper brings us into a meal where we celebrate with the cup of blessing and the bread of life. He gives us both medicine and food for our bodies and souls.

Baptism gives us different imagery and moves us to celebrate the washing away of sin and the resurrection of the soul to everlasting life. At the *Lord's table*, we eat the bread and drink the fruit of the vine.

In baptism our bodies are immersed in water, picturing our union with Christ and the cleansing of a guilty conscience. We demonstrate that we have been buried with Him in baptism and raised up to everlasting life.

Mixing them together we see the abundant mercies of God. The believer is offered bread, the fruit of the vine, cleansing, death to the old man, and resurrection to new life.

These miraculous acts of grace remind us that we are protected from what we deserved. We deserved a stone, a poison cup, a beating, and eternal death. Instead, we are given the opposite. These two ordinances proclaim the love of God for sinners. They are saturated in mercy.

THE LORD'S TABLE

Lead your children to see the rich theology of the blessing of the Lord's table. It is a physical symbol of the depths of the atonement. Matthew Henry, in his book on the Lord's Supper, stated it well:

> *"Fountains of life are here broken up, wells of salvation are here opened. The stone rolled away from the well's mouth. And you are called upon to come and draw water with joy. The well is deep, but this ordinance is easy to draw upon. Let us not forsake these living streams for the stagnant water."*[1]

---

1 Henry, M. (2005). *The Communicant's Companion: Instructions for the Right Receiving of the Lord's Supper* (p. 51). Birmingham, AL: Solid Ground Christian Books.

God designed this ordinance to teach us to "Taste and see that the Lord is good."

HERE ARE A FEW THINGS YOU OUGHT TO TEACH YOUR CHILDREN ABOUT THE LORD'S SUPPER

The Lord's Supper is *communion,* or a fellowship, a connection, a participation, a sharing. It is hard to find a more beautiful, compelling, and graphic depiction of the glory of the gospel.

- It is a *cup of blessing.* When Jesus took the bread and broke it, He "gave thanks" (Luke 22:17-19; Matt. 26:27). The Greek word for this is *Eucharesteo*, which means grace and joy. It is the word from which we get our English word, "Eucharist."
- It is *a supper,* a fellowship meal with Christ Himself illustrating the blessings of friendship with Christ (Luke 2:14-20).
- It is *a foretaste* of the marriage feast with Christ in heaven (Luke 22:16).
- It is a *remembrance* of Jesus Christ Himself and all He does and all He represents (1 Cor. 11:24).
- It is a *proclamation* of the Lord's death until He comes (1 Cor. 11:26).
- It is a *self-examination*, the first step of church discipline, searching our hearts for the remaining manifestations of sin (1 Cor. 11:28).
- It's a *confession* where we embrace the effectiveness of the body and the blood of Jesus Christ.
- It is a *covenant,* marking the inauguration of the new covenant (Luke 22:20).

Children should know in detail what the Lord's Supper is all about. If you are a Baptist (in contrast to a Presbyterian) and are waiting for your children to become new creatures, you must still teach them the meanings of the ordinances. When

149

they are finally born again, having entered the kingdom of heaven, having passed from death to life and from darkness to light, they will know the meaning more than ever. Until that time, make sure they know about the practices, as well as the joys, promises, and assurances that are being communicated in the ordinances.

BAPTISM

Baptism tells the story of the death and resurrection of Christ. It is a celebration of union with Christ in His death, resurrection, and newness of life. You act out physically what has already happened to you spiritually. The Second London Baptist Confession of 1689 describes it as, "a sign of his fellowship with him, in his death and resurrection; of his being engrafted into him; of remission of sins; and of giving up into God, through Jesus Christ, to live and walk in newness of life" (Chapter 29).

Think of the joy it was for all of those to experience resurrection to life as Paul explained to the Christians in Rome.

> "Or do you not know that as many of us as were baptized into Christ Jesus were baptized into His death? Therefore we were buried with Him through baptism into death, that just as Christ was raised from the dead by the glory of the Father, even so, we also should walk in newness of life" (Rom. 6:3-4).

Remember, you are a tour guide for joy as you explain this ordinance.

Help your children try to imagine what it was like for the 3,000 converted on the day of Pentecost (Acts 2:41); for Lydia, the devout, tenderhearted woman from Phillipi

(Acts 16:13-14); for the jailer in Philippi, hardened by the realities of crime, rebellion, and blood, who was baptized immediately after he believed (Acts 16:26-30); for the Ethiopian official who was struck to the heart by reading the prophet Isaiah on the road to Gaza (Acts 8:26-40). Try to imagine what it was like for the early Christians in the city of Corinth to become "baptized into one body," receiving a new family (1 Cor. 12:13).

In baptism we are not nailed to the cross for our sins. Rather, it illustrates that we are washed of our filth.

These ordinances are for public declarations of comfort and joy. In them, we see the magnitude of our sin, but we are not left to wallow there. While they remind us of our sin, they simultaneously take us out of the despondency to lift us up out of the pit.

Make sure you come alongside your children to help them grasp the beauties of these ordinances. God has given you treasures in these two ordinances. In the Lord's Supper, He gives "the cup of blessing which we bless." In baptism, He says, "But you were washed, but you were sanctified, but you were justified in the name of the Lord Jesus and by the Spirit of our God" (1 Cor. 6:11).

DISCUSSION

- Are you as parents born again, and have you been baptized in the name of the Lord Jesus?
- Discuss the various aspects of the imagery of baptism and the Lord's Supper and consider how you might make these things more exciting to your children.

AT <u>THE</u> GATES <u>OF</u> EVERLASTING JOY

*"So the ransomed of the L*ORD *shall return, and come to Zion with singing, with everlasting joy on their heads. They shall obtain joy and gladness; sorrow and sighing shall flee away" (Isa. 51:11).*

P arents, you are tour guides at the gates of everlasting joy. Go for it. Give it your whole heart. Don't miss the treasures. As a great tour guide, you need to help your children see the opportunities there. Help them experience the beautiful things God has in store for families who prioritize gathering with the redeemed in local churches. What is in store is better than what your children could gain from their sports or hobbies.

There is something you must first understand about God, His Kingdom and His church. Everything He does for His chosen people in the world is to sweep them into everlasting joy. He flung these doors open on the cross.

Jesus tells us that everything He said was so that His joy would "remain in you, and that your joy may be full" (John 15:11). Songwriters can't stop writing about it. It is the joy that makes wounded sinners sing, "We have heard the joyful sound, Jesus saves! Jesus saves! Spread the tidings all around, Jesus saves, Jesus saves." This is why the psalmist said, "Blessed are the people who know the joyful sound!" (Ps. 89:15).

When David said, "I was glad when they said unto me, 'let us go into the house of the Lord,'" he was referring to the joys of meeting with God in the Temple. This is a foretaste of heaven.

Parents, don't underestimate what God has done in giving you the local church. He did it for your joy. He did it to give you a thousand reasons to love the Lord. Your children need to know that.

THE GATES OF ZION

God stated His priorities when He said, "The Lord loves the gates of Zion more than all the dwellings of Jacob" (Ps. 87:2). God is telling us that He thinks more highly of the people of God gathering together to worship Him than of worship in families. Mt. Zion is a symbol of the place where God dwells among His people as they gather together to worship Him. The psalm ends with a sense of the joys that await those who gather, "All my springs are in you." Here is a brief explanation from the MacArthur Study Bible:

> *"Springs is a metaphor for the source of joyful blessings. Eternal salvation, including the death and resurrection of Christ, is rooted in Jerusalem. The prophets also tell of a literal fountain flowing from the temple in Jerusalem which will water the surrounding land" (Joel 3:18; Ezra 47:1-12).*

This does not minimize the massive importance of the worship of God in families. Saturating your homes with the Word of God, when you "sit in your house, when you walk by the way, when you lie down, and when you rise up," is one of the most powerful things you can do (Deut. 6:7).

THE JOY OF THE WHOLE EARTH

God has given us many ways to describe what it means for the people of God to come together corporately. The meaning of "Zion" in the Bible is rich and deep and wide. It refers to the

Lord's house, "His Holy hill," and "the city of God." It is the place where "He has dwelt" and "will reign" (Ps. 74:2; Isa. 24:23; Ps. 2:6; Ps. 87:2-3) and the house where His "glory dwells" (Ps. 26:8). It often refers to God's spiritual kingdom alive in the church (Heb. 12:22; Isa. 60:14). It is often associated with the people of God as in Psalm 97:8, "Zion hears and is glad, and the daughters of Judah rejoice because of your Judgments O Lord." Zion even refers to Christ Himself (1 Pet. 2:6). He tells us that the gatherings of Zion are "the joy of the whole earth." The theme running through these Scripture texts is joy and gladness.

FAMILIES TOGETHER IN WORSHIP

God loves to gather families together for worship. He loves it so much that He sent His Son to suffer on the cross to achieve it. That great Messianic Psalm 22, which prophesies Christ's suffering, makes this perfectly clear. His sufferings are often misunderstood as a dark and depressing failure. This is not the case. On "Good Friday," when Jesus cried out on the cross, "My God my God, why have you forsaken Me?," He was bearing our sin. However, He was simultaneously securing the victory that makes families sing for joy:

> *"All the ends of the world shall remember and turn to the Lord, and all the families of the nations shall worship before You" (Ps. 22:27).*

You have to read the whole of Psalm 22 to understand what Jesus meant when He said, "Why have you forsaken Me?" This is the "joy that was set before Him" (Heb. 12:2). This is why we call it "Good Friday." A most wonderful thing happened on that day. Without Christ's suffering on that day, we could not be saved—your children could not be saved. There would be no church in which to celebrate our freedom

155

from sin. We would be left forsaken. But He was forsaken for our transgressions, so that we would never be forsaken. This is wonderful news. This is "the joyful sound."

TOUR GUIDES STIRRING UP GLADNESS

This is how local churches are designed to stir up gladness in the Lord. This kind of gladness springs from family members as a result of hearing the "Praises of the Lord, and His strength" (Ps. 78:4). I want to encourage you to develop a family culture where you all say with your whole hearts, "I was glad when they said unto me, let us go into the house of the Lord."

All of this is launched out of a heart which says, "We will not hide them from our children." Hide what? The treasures of the gospel! It is such a wonderful thing to put your hand to the plow and say, "When I am old and grayheaded, O God, do not forsake me, until I declare Your strength to this generation, Your power to everyone who is to come" (Ps. 71:18).

THE NORMAL CHRISTIAN LIFE

Charles Spurgeon, preaching from John 16, said:

> *"Joy is the normal condition of a believer. His proper state, his healthy state is that of happiness and gladness... 'rejoice in the Lord' is the precept given to us over and over again... Broadly speaking the general condition of God's people is one of joy.... 'Happy are you, O Israel.' True Christians are the happiest people under heaven. They have many sorrows... but they are sorrowful yet always rejoicing."*[1]

---

1   Spurgeon, C. (1897). *The Metropolitan Tabernacle Pulpit Sermons, Vol. XLIII* (p. 325). London, England: Passmore & Alabaster

GOD'S DESIGN

We build the city of God on earth, in the family, and in the church in order to picture and prepare for everlasting joy. This is the purpose of all church life and family life. We do family worship so the children would see, in God's own words, what it's like to know Him. We show them how wonderful it is to eat His bread, graze in His green pastures and drink the fruit of His vine.

We order our churches according to the biblical patterns, because the patterns of singing, preaching, prayer, and soaking in the glory of Jesus is what God has designed for His children—even the little ones. Especially the little ones. The gospel opens all these doors to the beauties of everlasting joy. These beauties are seen and experienced in local churches. This is part of what making disciples of Jesus Christ looks like.

What does it take to show our children true treasure? What do we need to do to help them sing the praises of the Lord, teach them the ways of gladness, and pave the way for everlasting joy?

DULL TOUR GUIDES

Parents are tour guides. Not all tour guides have the same effect on the tourists. Some are interesting and some are dull. Some are enlightening and some are boring. Don't be a boring tour guide in the church of Jesus Christ. There are delectable delights waiting to be tasted, because the church is a cornucopia of opportunity. All good leaders have this in common: they help their followers see the glory of what they do. They are inspiration machines.

God has given you the resources to be an engaging tour guide.

One more thing. When the rain falls, and the winds blow and the storms of life break upon your family, make sure your house is built on the rock. Make sure you have fortified your children so that they can stand up to the wind and the rain that is coming. It is coming! It is your job to prepare them. There is no better preparation than a lifetime of saturation in the means of grace within a local church. Make sure they have had the opportunity to "offer sacrifices of joy" (Ps. 27:6), the "sacrifice of praise" (Heb. 13:6), and to "behold the beauty of the Lord" (Ps. 27:4). I pray that your family will "come to Zion with singing, with everlasting joy on your heads" (Isa. 51:11).

DISCUSSION

- Are you building a family culture of thoughts and feelings of joy for your local church?
- Are there things you have been doing that dampen family joy at home or for your local church?

FOR MORE ON EVERLASTING JOY

John 16:20-24; John 15:11; John 17:13; Rom. 15:13; Prov. 16:29; Ps. 28:7; Ps. 68:3; Neh. 8:10; Hab. 3:17; Ps. 118:24; Ps. 89:16; Ps. 132:16; Ps. 40:16; Ps. 16:11; Isa. 12:3; Isa. 35:10; Isa. 65:14; Isa. 66:14.